SIGNATURE SERIES

ELITE SWIM 24
WORKOUT

6 MONTHS OF DAILY SWIM WORK OUTS!

KALINOWSKI

Check out *the other Elite Swim Workout signature series books:*

ELITE SWIMMING WORKOUT 2019-2020
ELITE SWIMMING WORKOUT 2019-2020 METERS Edition
ELITE SWIM WORKOUT 21
ELITE SWIM WORKOUT 22
ELITE SWIM WORKOUT 23

Check out *other books:*

The Wolves of War

For my two lovely daughters who have embarked on their own swimming journey.
To all the coaches who I've worked with over the years, who have inspired many of the sets
in here.

AUTHORS NOTE

Welcome to Elite Swim Workout 24!

New year, a new you!

This years edition is the biggest redesign we've done to Elite Swim Workout since its inception. We've listened to your commentary about formatting and making everything cleaner, and easier to understand, and we listened.
Each workout now has clear sections in tables, dividing each set into: WARMUP, SPRINT, DISTANCE, MID DISTANCE or MAIN SET.
That's not all either.
On top of that, we know some coaches love looking at the entire week's worth of sets at once. And so, we have the "week snapshot". An entire's weeks worth of sets and workouts one one page. Further, we've also labeled each series of workouts pending which week they correlate too. Weeks 1-27.
We hope all these changes are to your liking!

AUTHORS BIO AND INTRO

Ive now been swimming for 29 years.

Throughout the years, I have practiced with all types of people and teams. Ive
trained and competed against Olympians and gold medalists, triathletes, state champions,
and cut my teeth against some of the fastest swimmers on the planet.
As a teenager, I was a full-on distance swimmer, winning state championships in the
1650. I eventually moved over to mid-D, setting multiple school records in events like 500 ,
200, and the 100.

In college, I joined a D1 school, and transitioned to full time sprinting, breaking numerous school
records (50,100, 200 and all the relays), and eventually becoming a league champion in the 50, and
even setting the 50 free record for the meet (which was then broken again soon after).
After graduating in 2012, I took a short break, before getting back into it and competing
again at the US Open in 2013.

Swimming is a hard sport, there is no getting around that. Part of the difficulty is the
amount of time that needs to be invested to keep up with ones training. After starting a
family, I found it was quite difficult to find the time to make it to Masters workouts, which
led me to train quite a bit by myself.
That is where this book comes in.
The resources out there are very limited when it comes to workouts for top tier
athletes, especially if you are swimming with no coach. Most training regimes you find
online feel quite random and its impossible to find an Olympic-level workout for
the seasoned swimmer.
That being said, this doesn't *have* to be for an Olympic-caliber athlete. If you find the
times are too fast, use the slower interval listed on the sheet. If its still too much, the intervals
can easily be adjusted by adding 10-20 seconds per set.

All in all, what you'll find here is a season's worth of workouts, for the motivated
athlete. Each has been custom crafted, and they are all reminiscent of the top-tier workouts
I experienced throughout my college career.

As usual, each training session is designed for a specific day for the 2023-24 college season, and
maintains a single day off per week (Sunday).

Hope you enjoy!

GLOSSARY of TERMS

FR: Freestyle
BK: BackStroke
BR: BreastStroke
FL: Butterfly

JMI: Just Make the Interval
SKIMPS: Swim, Kick, IM, Pull, Swim
200 SKIMPS means 200 swim, 200 kick, 200 IM, 200 Pull, 200 Swim

Choice: Your choice of Stroke
Stroke: Your main Stroke
IM: Individual Medley (Fly, Back, Breast, Free)
IMO: see above
RIMO: Reverse IM Order (Free, Breast, Back, Fly)

Broken: Break the distance per instruction.
(Broken 100 - Break at the 50 for the specified amount)
(Broken 200 - Break at the 100 for the specified amount)
(Broken 500 - Break after each 100 for the specified amount)

Negative split: Second half must be faster than the first half
Build: Slowly raise effort and speed as you go
Accelerate: Max effort breakout + 4 Strokes, rest of the length is easy
Underwater: Swim the length underwater with no breathe

DPS- Distance per Stroke. Try to minimize your stroke count.
BP- Breathing pattern (BP - 5 means one breath every 5 Strokes)
RB- Restriction Breathing (RB:2 Means 2 breaths total for the length)
RB:0- No breath this length

(Multiple intervals)
3:40/4:00/4:20 - - Choose one interval for the set that works for you.
Left most interval is the most challenging.

3 x {ITEM} - The item in the brackets will be done 3 times

(1:00)- One minute rest

Reduce:1 - reduce Stroke count by alloted amount per length.

Best Average: Maintain the fastest speed you can for the duration of the set. For example, 5x100 best average - If the best you can hold is 1:00, then hold that time for the full 5 x 100's

Goal Pace: Take either your goal time for the specific event, or your best time for the event and add the specified amount to it to get your time.

These below correlate to your heart rate, but its easier to understand by effort/ speed:

Clear: 0% Easy pace

White: 25% Casual effort

Pink: 50% Half effort

Red: 60-70% Hard effort

Blue: 80-90% Fast pace

Max: 100% MAX pace

EXAMPLE SET:

4 x 200 Free/Back @ 3:00 /3:30 -Four 200's, your choice of Free or back. You pick the interval for the whole set, either 3:00 or 3:30

Example Drills

Descend, D1-4 - Descend your time. D1-4 means the 4th one should be the fastest

Ascend: Start fast and then slow down

Accelerate: Start from flags - max speed until halfway and then easy

Catchup-(Freestyle, BackStroke). Start in streamline position with a steady kick. Perform a front crawl Stroke where your hands touch before the next
hand begins its motion

Heads up - (Freestyle) Keep your head out of the water

Fingertip - (Freestyle) Drag your fingertips on the surface of the water

Single arm - (Freestyle, Butterfly, Back) Only use One arm. Reverse arm on the length back

2K, 1P - (BreastStroke) - Two kicks for every One Pull

Breast w/ DK (BreastStroke) - BreastStroke with Dolphin kick

Breast w/ FK (BreastStroke) - BreastStroke with Flutter kick

Double arm back (BackStroke) - BackStroke with concurrent double arm pull

Fist (Freestyle): Freestyle with a fist rather than an open palm

HOW TO READ THE WORKOUT

WEEK 1	Fri Sep 01 2023

WARMUP	2 x 300 Pull/ @ 3:45/3:50
	5 x 100 Pull (50 Free/50 Non-Free) @ 1:30/1:40
	2 x {
	   4 x 50 Fist Drill @ 1:10
	   2 x 25 Build to Pink @ :30
	}

SPRINT	6 x 100 Kick @ 1:50 8 x 100 Paddle w/Pull Buoy @ :15 rest 6 x 50 odds: Red @ 1:00 evens: blue @ 1:00 200 clear 10 x 50 @ 1:30 MAX PACE
DISTANCE	1 x 400 FR/Non-FR by 100 4 x 100 IM (2) White (2) Pink @ 1:50 4 x 50 JMI @ :45/:50 (2:00) 1 x 300 FR/Non-FR by 50 3 x 100 IM (2) Pink (1) Red @ 1:10 4 x 50 JMI @ :40/:45 (1:00) 1 x 200 FR/Non-FR by 100 2 x 100 JMI Red-Blue @ 1:50 4 x 50 JMI Dolphin kick @ :55/1:00
MID-DISTANCE	8 x 75 @ 1:15 Odds: Work Turns Evens: Work Finish 1 x 600 (3 x 100 White/100 Red) 3 x (400 + 100 easy) D 1-3 3 x (200 + 50 easy) D 1-3

i. Everyone does the warmup set together

ii. After that, pick ONE section which will be your "main" set for the workout.

iii. For instance, a sprinter would do the WARMUP and then do the SPRINT set and call it a day

iv. A distance swimmer would do the WARMUP and do the DISTANCE set and for their workout

v. A Mid-D swimmer would do the WARMUP and do the Mid-D set and for their workout

Equipment needed:
Swimsuit: Public swim pools strongly frown on nude workouts.
Drag-suit: I swore by one. Slows you down by a small amount. Drag-suit comes off when its time to get serious.
Cap: Keeps your loose hair out of the pool.
Water Bottle w/water: Hydration is key.
Board: Everyone's favorite mid-workout surfboard. Used for kicking sets. And there'll be lots of 'em!
Fins: Get a size that fits, and that won't fall off when you kick hard or do flip turns. I prefer the longer ones over the short fins.
Paddles: Expands the size of your hands, to work on your pull. Get a size that works for your hand, I wouldn't recommend going overboard with the monster sized ones.
Buoy: To put in between your legs and to stop kicking, and for rotations. Bread and butter of swim workouts.
Chutes: Strap it to your waist and significantly increase the resistance you feel in the water. Must have for sprinters.

*All the of the workouts are designed for a standard 25 Yard pool

SEPTEMBER   ELITE SWIM WORKOUT '24   WEEK 1

Monday	Tuesday	Wednesday	Thursday	Friday	Saturday

				2 x 300 Pull @ 3:45/3:50
				5 x 100 Pull (50 Free/50 Non-Free)
				
				2 x {
				  4 x 50 Fist Drill @ 1:10
				  2 x 25 Build to Pink @ :30
				}
				
				SPRINT
				
				6 x 100 Kick @ 1:50
				8 x 100 Paddle w/Pull Buoy @ :15 rest
				6 x 50
				odds: Red @ 1:00
				evens: blue @ 1:00
				
				200 clear
				10 x 50 @ 1:30 MAX PACE
				
				DISTANCE
				
				1 x 400 FR/Non-FR by 100
				4 x 100 IM (2) White (2) Pink @ 1:50
				4 x 50 JMI @ :45/:50
				(2:00)
				1 x 300 FR/Non-FR by 50
				3 x 100 IM (2) Pink (1) Red @ 1:10
				4 x 50 JMI @ :40/:45
				(1:00)
				1 x 200 FR/Non-FR by 100
				2 x 100 JMI Red-Blue @ 1:50
				4 x 50 JMI Dolphin kick @ :55/1:00
				
				MID-DISTANCE
				
				8 x 75 @ 1:15
				Odds: Work Turns
				Evens: Work Finish
				1 x 600 (3 x 100 White/100 Red)
				3 x (400 + 100 easy)
				D 1-3
				3 x (200 + 50 easy)
				D 1-3
				5 x 100 Blue + 50 easy
				3 x 200 Blue + 100 easy
					200 SKIMPS
					6 x 50 IMO @ 1:00
					
					8 x 50 @ :50
					odds: build into first wall, great turn
					evens: build into finish, great finish
					
					2 x {
					  4 x 25 (drill,build,drill,MAX) @ :40
					}
					
					IM
					3 x 300 IMO by 75's@ :20 Rest
					4 x 100 IM JMI @ 1:20/1:30
					(:30)
					4 x 100 IMO @ 1:30/1:40
					Descend
					(1:00)
					8 x 50 Hold Goal Pace 200 +1 Same Stroke @ 1:00

WEEK 1	Fri Sep 01 2023

WARMUP	2 x 300 Pull/ @ 3:45/3:50
	5 x 100 Pull (50 Free/50 Non-Free) @ 1:30/1:40
	2 x {
	    4 x 50 Fist Drill @ 1:10
	    2 x 25 Build to Pink @ :30
	}

SPRINT	6 x 100 Kick @ 1:50 8 x 100 Paddle w/Pull Buoy @ :15 rest 6 x 50 odds: Red @ 1:00 evens: blue @ 1:00 200 clear 10 x 50 @ 1:30 MAX PACE
DISTANCE	1 x 400 FR/Non-FR by 100 4 x 100 IM (2) White (2) Pink @ 1:50 4 x 50 JMI @ :45/:50 (2:00) 1 x 300 FR/Non-FR by 50 3 x 100 IM (2) Pink (1) Red @ 1:10 4 x 50 JMI @ :40/:45 (1:00) 1 x 200 FR/Non-FR by 100 2 x 100 JMI Red-Blue @ 1:50 4 x 50 JMI Dolphin kick @ :55/1:00
MID-DISTANCE	8 x 75 @ 1:15 Odds: Work Turns Evens: Work Finish 1 x 600 (3 x 100 White/100 Red) 3 x (400 + 100 easy) D 1-3 3 x (200 + 50 easy) D 1-3 5 x 100 Blue + 50 easy 3 x 200 Blue + 100 easy

WEEK 1	Sat Sep 02 2023

WARMUP	200 SKIMPS
	6 x 50 IMO @ 1:00
	
	8 x 50 @ :50
	odds: build into first wall, great turn
	evens: build into finish, great finish
	
	2 x {
	   4 x 25 (drill,build,drill,MAX) @ :40
	}

MAIN SET	IM 3 x 300 IMO by 75's@ :20 Rest 4 x 100 IM JMI @ 1:20 / 1:30 (:30) 4 x 100 IMO @ 1:30 / 1:40 Descend (1:00) 8 x 50 Hold Goal Pace 200 +1 Same Stroke @ 1:00

SEPTEMBER   ELITE SWIM WORKOUT '24   WEEK 2

Monday	Tuesday	Wednesday	Thursday	Friday	Saturday

1 x 200 BackStroke
1 x 200 Fly
1 x 200 Free
 	
SPRINT
 	
6 x 12.5 MAX Breakouts
12 x 50 Free Red @ :50
 	
1 x 300 White @ 3:50
4 x (100 + 25) Build @ 2:10
Last 25 red 2 breaths
(1:00)
5 x (50 + 25) Build @ 1:40
Last 25 blue 2 breaths
(2:00)
1 x 300 Pink @ 4:00
 	
4 x 50 MAX @ 4:00
 	
DISTANCE
 	
1 x 500 White
5 x 100 @ 1:05/1:10/1:15
 	
1 x 400 White
4 x 100 @ 1:05/1:10/1:15
 	
1 x 300 White
3 x 100 @ 1:05/1:10/1:15
 	
1 x 200 White
2 x 100 @ 1:05/1:10/1:15
 	
MID-DISTANCE
 	
4 x 200 2:40/2:50
Descend Each 200 + 25 Blue
(1:00)
4 x 300 @ 4:10/4:20
Each 300 - 100 Pull no buoy, 100 Build, 100
MAX Kick
(1:00)
10 x 100 @ 1:25/1:30
Hold Best Average
(2:00)
8 x 100 @ 1:10
	3 x 200 Free
	1 x 100 Kick Fly
	3 x 100 Freestyle
	
	SPRINT
	
	6 x 75 w/fins (drill/swim/drill) @ 1:10
	6 x 75 w/fins (underwater kick/swim/dolphin on back) @ 1:15
	
	IM
	4 x 200
	White-Pink-Red-Blue
	(1:00)
	odds: Free Descend
	Evens: Stroke D2-8 to MAX
	Cooldown
		300 Kick
		200 Free
		4 x 100 IM @ 20 rest
		
		4 x 75 (25 fist drill/25 swim/25 build) @ 1:20
		8 x 50 (25 kick no board/25 swim) @ 1:00
		
		SPRINT
		
		2 x (10 x 50 @ 1:30) ALL OUT MAX
		Cooldown
		DISTANCE
		
		4 x 50 Kick no board RED @ :50
		(:30)
		4 x 200 @ 2:10/2:20
		White-Pink- (2) Red
		4 x 50 Kick no board BLUE@ :50
		(1:00)
		8 x 100 JMI @ 1:05/1:10
		
		MID-DISTANCE
		
		3 x 500 (White/Pink/Red)
		3 x 400 (White/Pink/Red)
		(2:00)
		4 x 200 (White/Pink/Red/Blue)
		4 x 100 Best Average
			1 x 800 Free RB4
			1 x 100 Kick
			
			4 x 200 @ 2:30/2:40
			odds: BP: 3,5 by 100
			evens: BP: 3,7 by 50
			(2:00)
			3 x 300 w/fins @ 3:15/3:30
			odds: DPS – lowest Stroke count
			evens: kick ½ underwater on each wall
			(2:00)
			IM
			4 x 200 IM @ 2:45/3:00
			Descend
			
			8 x 100 IMO w/fins @ 1:20/1:30
			
			8 x 50 @ :45/:50
			1-4 #1 Stroke, 4-8 Worst Stroke
				1 x 400 (200 Free/200 Non-Free)
				1 x 300 Kick
				1 x 200 RIMO (drill fly)
				
				1 x 300 Scull
				
				6 x 50 Kick @ 1:00
				1 x 300 easy kick
				8 x 50 Kick w/fins @ :30/:35
				
				8 x 25 Fist @ :30
				4 x 25 Build @ :30
				4 x 25 MAX @ :30
				
				SPRINT
				
				1 x 500 (200 Free White/200 Free Pink/100 Free Build Finish)
				1 x 300 (150 Free White/150 Non-Free) @
				4 x 50 Kick Build to Pink @ 1:00
				4 x 50 fist drill @ 1:10
				8 x 25 build Stroke @ :40
				
				DISTANCE
				
				3 x 200 IM @ 3:00/3:10
				3 x 200 (Kick no Board/Kick board /Choice)
				(1:00)
				4 x 25 underwater kick @ :45
				4 x 25 underwater with arms @ :40
				4 x 25 (1/2 way underwater MAX kick + breakout/easy) @ :30
				(1:00)
				3 x 200 IM :30 sec
				6 x 100 JMI @ 1:05/1:10/1:15
				(1:00)
				2 x 100 JMI @ 1:00/1:05/1:10
				
				MID-DISTANCE
				
				2 x {
				1 x 600 Red
				(2:00)
				1 x 400 Red
				(2:00)
				1 x 200 Red
				(2:00)
				}
				
				1 x 300 cool down
					1 x 400 Free
					1 x 300 Non-Free
					2 x 200 Kick
					4 x 100 IM (drill fly)
					8 x 50 w/chutes @ 1:10
					odds: (25 no breath/25 Pink)
					evens: (25 Pink/25 Red)
					6 x 25 Build @ :30
					
					2 x {
					8 x 50 Kick #1 Stroke D1-4, 5-8 to MAX
					1 x 400 Kick no board
					}
					8 x 100 (25 white/50 RB: 5 /25 Pink) @ 1:30
					
					3 x {
					1 x 75 MAX + :30 rest + 50 MAX from push
					}
					2 x {
					1 x 50 MAX + :30 rest + 25 MAX from push
					}

15

WEEK 2	Mon Sep 04 2023
WARMUP	1 x 200 BackStroke 1 x 200 Fly 1 x 200 Free
SPRINT	6 x 12.5 MAX Breakouts 12 x 50 Free Red @ :50 1 x 300 White @ 3:50 4 x (100 + 25) Build @ 2:10 Last 25 red 2 breaths (1:00) 5 x (50 + 25) Build @ 1:40 Last 25 blue 2 breaths (2:00) 1 x 300 Pink @ 4:00 4 x 50 MAX @ 4:00
DISTANCE	1 x 500 White 5 x 100 @ 1:05/1:10/1:15 1 x 400 White 4 x 100 @ 1:05/1:10/1:15 1 x 300 White 3 x 100 @ 1:05/1:10/1:15 1 x 200 White 2 x 100 @ 1:05/1:10/1:15
MID-DISTANCE	4 x 200 @ 2:40/2:50 Descend Each 200 + 25 Blue (1:00) 4 x 300 @ 4:10/4:20 Each 300 - 100 Pull no buoy, 100 Build , 100 MAX Kick (1:00) 10 x 100 @ 1:25/1:30 Hold Best Average (2:00) 8 x 100 @ 1:10

WEEK 2	Tue Sep 05 2023
WARMUP	3 x 200 Free 1 x 100 Kick Fly 3 x 100 Freestyle 6 x 75 w/fins (drill/swim/drill) @ 1:10 6 x 75 w/fins (underwater kick/swim/dolphin on back) @ 1:15
MAIN SET	 IM 4 x 200 White-Pink-Red-Blue (1:00) 2 x (300 + 100 white) Pink-Red (1:30) 8 x (100 + 100 white) odds: Free Descend Evens: Stroke D2-8 to MAX Cooldown

WEEK 2	Wed Sep 06 2023
WARMUP	300 Kick 200 Free 4 x 100 IM @ :20 rest 4 x 75 (25 fist drill/25 swim/25 build) @ 1:20 8 x 50 (25 kick no board/25 swim) @ 1:00
SPRINT	2 x (10 x 50 @ 1:30) ALL OUT MAX Cooldown
DISTANCE	4 x 50 Kick no board RED @ :50 (:30) 4 x 200 @ 2:10/2:20 White-Pink-(2) Red 4 x 50 Kick no board BLUE@ :50 (1:00) 8 x 100 JMI @ 1:05/1:10
MID-DISTANCE	3 x 500 (White/Pink/Red) 3 x 400 (White/Pink/Red) (2:00) 4 x 200 (White/Pink/Red/Blue) 4 x 100 Best Average

WEEK 2	Thu Sep 07 2023
WARMUP	1 x 800 Free RB4 1 x 100 Kick 4 x 200 @ 2:30/2:40 odds: BP: 3,5 by 100 evens: BP: 3,7 by 50 (2:00) 3 x 300 w/fins @ 3:15/3:30 odds: DPS – lowest Stroke count evens: kick ½ underwater on each wall (2:00)
MAIN SET	IM 4 x 200 IM @ 2:45/3:00 Descend 8 x 100 IMO w/fins @ 1:20/1:30 8 x 50 @ :45/:50 1-4 #1 Stroke, 4-8 Worst Stroke

WEEK 2	Fri Sep 08 2023
WARMUP	1 x 400 (200 Free / 200 Non-Free) 1 x 300 Kick 1 x 200 RIMO (drill fly) 1 x 300 Scull 6 x 50 Kick @ 1:00 1 x 300 easy kick 8 x 50 Kick w/fins @ :30/:35 8 x 25 Fist @ :30 4 x 25 Build @ :30 4 x 25 MAX @ :30
SPRINT	1 x 500 (200 Free White / 200 Free Pink / 100 Free Build Finish) 4 x 50 Kick Build to Pink @ 1:00 1 x 300 (150 Free White / 150 Non-Free) @ 4 x 50 fist drill @ 1:10 8 x 25 build Stroke @ :40
DISTANCE	3 x 200 IM @ 3:00/3:10 3 x 200 (Kick no Board / Kick board / Choice) (1:00) 4 x 25 underwater kick @ :45 4 x 25 underwater with arms @ :40 4 x 25 (1/2 way underwater MAX kick + breakout/easy) @ :30 (1:00) 3 x 200 IM :30 sec 6 x 100 JMI @ 1:05/1:10/1:15 (1:00) 2 x 100 JMI @ 1:00/1:05/1:10

MID-DISTANCE	2 x {
	   1 x 600 Red
	   (2:00)
	   1 x 400 Red
	   (2:00)
	   1 x 200 Red
	   (2:00)
	    }
	1 x 300 cool down

WEEK 2	Sat Sep 09 2023
WARMUP	1 x 400 Free 1 x 300 Non-Free 2 x 200 Kick 4 x 100 IM (drill fly) 8 x 50 w/chutes @ 1:10 odds: (25 no breath/25 Pink) evens: (25 Pink/25 Red) 6 x 25 Build @ :30

MAIN SET	2 x {
	   8 x 50 Kick #1 Stroke D1-4 , 5-8 to MAX
	   1 x 400 Kick no board
	}
	8 x 100 (25 white/50 RB: 5 /25 Pink) @ 1:30
	3 x {
	   1 x 75 MAX + :30 rest + 50 MAX from push
	}
	2 x {
	   1 x 50 MAX + :30 rest + 25 MAX from push
	}

SEPTEMBER   ELITE SWIM WORKOUT '24   WEEK 3

Monday	Tuesday	Wednesday	Thursday	Friday	Saturday
1 x 600 (200 Free/200 BK/200 Choice) 6 x 50 drill/swim @ 1:00	1 x 400 IM 1 x 200 Kick with board 2 x 100 Freestyle	600 Free 3 x 100 Kick w/Board 10 x 100 IM Order @ :15 rest	200 SKIMPS 8 x 50 @ 1:00 odds: RB.1 evens: RB.3	3 x 300 #1 Free #2 Back #2 (150 Kick/150 Swim choice)	2 x 300 DPS @ 4:00 5 x 100 (3) White (2) Pink @ 1:30
6 x 75 (Kick/drill/swim) @ 1:10 8 x 25 @ :30 odds: drill / evens: stroke	50 Kick @ :10 rest 100 Free @ :10 rest 200 non-Free @ :10 rest 300 Kick @ :10 rest 200 Fin Swim @ :10 rest 100 Free @ :10 rest 50 Worst Stroke @ :10 rest	8 x 50 (25 Drill/25 Swim Stroke) @ 1:00	1 x 400 Build into each turn, breakout with no breath 1 x 300 Stroke	8 x 50 @ 1:00 Each one work one flip turns pushing off on back 4 x 100 JMI @ 1:10/1:15 #1-2 Neg Split (White/Red) #2-4 DPS	2 x 300 #1 Scull #2 (BK/Breast/Scull) by 100's
SPRINT 4 x 125 @ 1:50 6 x 25 accelerate @ :30		2 x 4 x 50 Catchup @ 1:10	3 x 300 pull @ 4:00 3 x 200 Ascend @ 2:40 3 x 100 Descend @ 1:20 3 x 50 max @ 1:00		8 x 75 (Kick-Drill-Swim) @ 1:10 Sprint 3 x 200 w/fins DPS @ 2:30 8 x 50 (25 Drill/ 25 build to max finish) @ .50

15 x 100 @ 1:30/1:40
#1-5 Negative Split (White/Blue)
#6-10 Descend to MAX
#7-15 Hold Best Average
	5 x 100 @ 1:30	SPRINT
		5 x {
		  200 Best Average @ /3:20
		  4 x 50 Avg. Best time 200 Pace @ 1:00
		  1:00 rest
		}
			3 x 200 cool down @ 15 sec rest	SPRINT
				8 x 100 IM@ 1:20
				3 x 300 @ 3:30/3:45
				Descend
				4 x 50 white @ 1:00
				3 x 200 @ 2:20/2:30
				Descend
				4 x 50 white @ 1:00
				DISTANCE
					2 x 200 @ 2:40
					4 x 50 Non-Free @ :50
					3 x 100 @ 1:20
					4 x 50 kick no board @ 1:00
					1 x 200 Kick Pink @ 4:00
					4 x 50 D 1-4 @ 1:00

1 x 300 2 x 200 @ 2:40 White Swim-White Kick	1 x 400 DPS @ 5:20 4 x 100 Choice 2 red/ 2 pink @ 1:50 (:30)	DISTANCE 1 x 1000 Broken (10 x 100 @ :20 rest) 1 x 500 Broken (10 x 50 @ :10 rest)		5 x (300 Best Average @ 3:50 + 3 x 100 Goal 500 Pace @ 1:30 + 1:00 rest)	8 x 25 Breakout
4 x 50 (Drill/Swim) @ 1:00 1x50 MAX from dive	1 x 400 pull @ 5:00 2 x 100 (2) White (1) Pink (:30)	MID-DISTANCE 2 x Broken 500s 3 x Broken 200s		MID-DISTANCE	
DISTANCE 3 x 500 @ 7:30/7:50 Bp 3-5-7-5-3 by 100's	1 x 400 pull @ 5:00 5 x 100 blue @ 1:20			4 x 25 (Drill/Build/Drill/Sprint) @ :40 3 x Broken 500s (:10 sec @ each 100)	
4 x 400 Paddle/Pull D 1-4 @ 5:20				Cooldown	
6 x 150 (FL/BK/BR) w/ fins @ 2:10					
6 x 150 @ 2:00 D 1-3, 4-6 to MAX					
MID-DISTANCE 3 x (500 + 100 easy) #1 Paddle/Pull - White #2 Paddle - Pink #3 Swim - Red					
3 x (300 + 100 easy) White-Pink-(2) Red (1:00) 1 x (200 MAX + 100 easy) 3 x (200 + 100 easy) Pink-Red-Blue (1:00) 1 x (100 MAX + 100 easy)					
2 x (100 + 50 easy) Pink-Red 1 x (50 MAX + 50 easy)					

WEEK 3	Mon Sep 11 2023
WARMUP	1 x 600 (200 Free/200 BK/200 Choice) 6 x 50 drill/swim @ 1:00 6 x 75 (Kick/drill/swim) @ 1:10 8 x 25 @ :30 odds: drill/ evens: stroke
SPRINT	4 x 125 @ 1:50 6 x 25 accelerate @ :30 15 x 100 @ 1:30/1:40 #1-5 Negative Split (White/Blue) #6-10 Descend to MAX #7-15 Hold Best Average 1 x 300 2 x 200 @ 2:40 White Swim-White Kick 4 x 50 (Drill/Swim) @ 1:00 1x50 MAX from dive
DISTANCE	3 x 500 @ 7:30/7:50 Bp 3-5-7-5-3 by 100's 4 x 400 Paddle/Pull D 1-4 @ 5:20 6 x 150 (FL/BK/BR) w/ fins @ 2:10 6 x 150 @ 2:00 D 1-3, 4-6 to MAX
MID-DISTANCE	3 x (500 + 100 easy) #1 Paddle/Pull - White #2 Paddle - Pink #3 Swim - Red 3 x (300 + 100 easy) White-Pink-(2) Red (1:00) 1 x (200 MAX + 100 easy) 3 x (200 + 100 easy) Pink-Red-Blue (1:00) 1 x (100 MAX + 100 easy) 2 x (100 + 50 easy) Pink-Red 1 x (50 MAX + 50 easy)

WEEK 3	Tue Sep 12 2023
WARMUP	1 x 400 IM 1 x 200 Kick with board 2 x 100 Freestyle 50 Kick @ :10 rest 100 Free @ :10 rest 200 non-Free @ :10 rest 300 Kick @ :10 rest 200 Fin Swim @ :10 rest 100 Free @ :10 rest 50 Worst Stroke @ :10 rest
MAIN SET	5 x 100 @ 1:30 1 x 400 DPS @ 5:20 4 x 100 Choice 2 red / 2 pink @ 1:50 (:30) 1 x 400 pull @ 5:00 2 x 100 (2) White (1) Pink (:30) 1 x 400 pull @ 5:00 5 x 100 blue @ 1:20

WEEK 3	Wed Sep 13 2023
WARMUP	600 Free 3 x 100 Kick w/Board 10 x 100 IM Order @ :15 rest 8 x 50 (25 Drill/25 Swim Stroke) @ 1:00 2 x 4 x 50 Catchup @ 1:10

SPRINT	5 x {
	   200 Best Average @ /3:20
	   4 x 50 Avg. Best time 200 Pace @ 1:00
	   1:00 rest
	}

DISTANCE	1 x 1000 Broken (10 x 100 @ :20 rest) 1 x 500 Broken (10 x 50 @ :10 rest)
MID-DISTANCE	2 x Broken 500s 3 x Broken 200s

WEEK 3	Thu Sep 14 2023
WARMUP	200 SKIMPS 8 x 50 @ 1:00 odds: RB:1 evens: RB:3 1 x 400 Build into each turn, breakout with no breath 1 x 300 Stroke
MAIN SET	 3 x 300 pull @ 4:00 3 x 200 Ascend @ 2:40 3 x 100 Descend @ 1:20 3 x 50 max @ 1:00 3 x 200 cool down @ 15 sec rest

WEEK 3	Fri Sep 15 2023
WARMUP	3 x 300 #1 Free #2 Back #2 (150 Kick/150 Swim choice) 8 x 50 @ 1:00 Each one work one flip turns pushing off on back 4 x 100 JMI @ 1:10/1:15 #1-2 Neg Split (White/Red) #2-4 DPS
SPRINT	8 x 100 IM@ 1:20 3 x 300 @ 3:30/3:45 Descend 4 x 50 white @ 1:00 3 x 200 @ 2:20/2:30 Descend 4 x 50 white @ 1:00
DISTANCE	5 x (300 Best Average @ 3:50 3 x 100 Goal 500 Pace @ 1:30 1:00 rest)
MID-DISTANCE	4 x 25 (Drill/Build/Drill/Drill/Sprint) @ :40 3 x Broken 500s (:10 sec @ each 100)

WEEK 3	Sat Sep 16 2023
WARMUP	2 x 300 DPS @ 4:00 5 x 100 (3) White (2) Pink @ 1:30 2 x 300 #1 Scull #2 (BK/Breast/Scull) by 100's 8 x 75 (Kick-Drill-Swim) @ 1:10 Sprint 3 x 200 w/fins DPS @ 2:30 8 x 50 (25 Drill/ 25 build to max finish) @ :50
MAIN SET	2 x 200 @ 2:40 4 x 50 Non-Free @ :50 3 x 100 @ 1:20 4 x 50 kick no board @ 1:00 1 x 200 Kick Pink @ 4:00 4 x 50 D 1-4 @ 1:00 8 x 25 Breakout

Monday	Tuesday	Wednesday	Thursday	Friday	Saturday

4 x 200
#1 White/Pink @ :20 rest
#2 IM order @ :30 rest
#3 Freestyle @ :30 rest
#4 No Breath in or out of walls
 	
1 x 400 (200 Kick/100 Free/100 Drill)
8x 100 paddle/pull @ 1:40/1:50
BP 5 by 100's
4 x 100 Paddle w/fast legs @ 1:10/1:20
 	
SPRINT
 	
3 x {
300 DPS @ 4:00
2 x 200 White-Pink @ 2:30
3 x 100 Choice @ 1:30
4 x 50 D 1-4 @ 1:00
}
 	
DISTANCE
12 x 25 (drill/build/drill/sprint) @ :40
3 x 200 White/Pink/Red @ 2:20/2:30/2:40
6 x 100 @ 1:25/1:30
odds: descend to MAX finish
evens: ascend MAX breakout
6 x 50 MAX each breakout off both walls @ 1:00
 	
MID-DISTANCE
 	
2 x Broken 500:
200 (White/Pink) @ :10 rest
100 Red @ 10 rest
100 Blue @ 10 rest
100 MAX
 	
1 x Broken 1650:
300 (Build) @ 10
200 White @ :10 rest
5 x 100 Best Avg @ :10 rest
300 (150 Pink/150 Red) :10
150 MAX
		1 x 400 Free
		1 x 300 Choice
		2 x 200 Kick
		3 x 100 IM
		
		6 x 100 DPS @ :50
		
		SPRINT
		
		4 x 200 @ 3:00
		(2) White (1) Pink
		(1:00)
		4 x 100 Pink – Red – Blue- MAX @ 1:20
		2 x {
		8 x 50 @ :50
		(:30)
		4 x 25 underwater @ :40
		}
		
		DISTANCE
		10 x (50+50 easy)
		500 – Hold 500 Goal pace – 2
		200 – Hold 200 Goal pace – 1
		5 x (100 + 100 easy)
		500 – Hold 500 Goal Pace
		200 – Hold 200 goal pace +1
		3 x (200 + 100 easy)
		D 1-3
		
		MID-DISTANCE
		12 x 75 (2 easy @ 1:10, 1 FAST @ 1:00)
		
		1 x 600 Pull @ 7:00/7:50
		4 x 75 Kick @ 1:20
		odds: White-Pink-Red
		Evens: Red-Pink-White
		(1:00)
		1 x 600 Pull @ 6:50/7:40
		4 x 100 Kick @ 1:30/1:40
		Descend to MAX start @ Pink
		(2:00)
		2 x 500 Swim @ 5:20/5:40
		(2:00)
		4 x 200 Swim w/fins @ 2:15
			4 x 200 @ :15 rest
			odds: Free
			evens: (50 back drill/50 Choice)
			
			10 x 25 Build each 25 to fast flip @ :50
			8 x 25 (12.5 underwater kick sprint/12.5 breakout MAX, easy) @ :30
			
			8 x 50 w/fins (12.5 underwater Kick Red/12.5 Swim no breath/25 white) @ 1:00
			(1:00)
			8 x 25 @ :40
			odds: Build
			evens: Accelerate
			
			5 x 100 Negative Split (50 White/50 Blue) @ 1:20
			Stroke - Free White/Stroke Blue
			(1:00)
			5 x 100 MAX Kick @ 2:00
			(3:00)
			5 x 100 D1-5 to MAX @ 1:20
			All Stroke
			(1:00)
			5 x 50 MAX Kick @ 1:20
			(3:00)
				4 x 200
				#1 Free #2 Back/Breast by 50's #3 100 BK/100 Choice #4 Free
				
				1 x 300 Kick
				2 x 200 (100 White/100 Red Kick @ 3:30
				6 x 50 D1-3 to Pink, 4-6 to MAX (start at White) @ 1:00
				
				6 x 100 Paddle w/Pull Buoy @ 1:20/1:30
				
				6 x 75 Descend @ 1:10
				odds: fly-back-breast
				evens: back-breast-free
				
				SPRINT
				
				400 Free
				200 Kick
				100 IM
				
				8 x 25 MAX on 1:00
				10 x 25 w/ chutes @ :45 Red
				10 x 25 x/ fins MAX underwater kick @ :30
				DISTANCE
				
				4 x (200 pull + 100 easy)
				Descend
				
				7 x (100 + 50 easy)
				#1-5 Goal 500 Pace
				#6-7 Hold #5 Time
				
				4 x (50 + 50 easy)
				All Fast
				
				MID-DISTANCE
				
				2 x 400 Paddle w/Pull Buoy @ 4:45/5:00
				3 x 200 IM :30 sec
				4 x 50 Free @ :40
				
				2 x 300 (150 Free/150 Non-Free) @
				4 x 100 Descend @ 1:30
				4 x 50 Free @ :40
				
				4 x 25s Max start + breakout
					1 x 600 (300 Free/200 Kick/100 Breast)
					
					1 x 500 Kick
					
					1 x 400 Kick
					4 x 100 Kick (50 pink/50 red) @ 1:50
					4 x 50 MAX Kick @ 1:00
					1 x 200 easy
					
					8 x 100 Build
					#1-4 w/fins @ 1:15/1:25
					#5-8 IM @ 1:30/1:40
					
					6 x 200 @ 2:55/3:10
					Descend1-3 Blue
					
					6 x 100 @ 1:20/1:30
					Descend 1-3
					Ascend 4-6
					
					4 x 100 Kick Red @ 1:30

29

WEEK 4	Mon Sep 18 2023
WARMUP	4 x 200 #1 White/Pink @ :20 rest #2 IM order @ :30 rest #3 Freestyle @ :10 rest #4 No Breath in or out of walls 1 x 400 (200 Kick/100 Free/100 Drill) 8x 100 paddle/pull @ 1:40/1:50 BP 5 by 100's 4 x 100 Paddle w/fast legs @ 1:10/1:20

SPRINT	3 x {
	   300 DPS @ 4:00
	   2 x 200 White-Pink @ 2:30
	   3 x 100 Choice @ 1:30
	   4 x 50 D 1-4 @ 1:00
	   }

DISTANCE	12 x 25 (drill/build/drill/sprint) @ :40 3 x 200 White/Pink/Red @ 2:20/2:30/2:40 6 x 100 @ 1:25/1:30 odds: descend to MAX finish evens: ascend MAX breakout 6 x 50 MAX each breakout off both walls @ 1:00
MID-DISTANCE	2 x Broken 500: 200 (White/Pink) @ :10 rest 100 Red @ :10 rest 100 Blue @ 10 rest 100 MAX 1 x Broken 1650: 300 (Build) @ :10 200 White @ :10 rest 5 x 100 Best Avg @ :10 rest 300 (150 Pink/150 Red) :10 150 MAX

WEEK 3	Tue Sep 19 2023
WARMUP	4 x 200 IM-NonFree-Free-Kick 4 x 50 @ 1:00 9 x 100 Paddle w/Pull Buoy @ 1:30 #1-3 White #4-6 Pink #7-9 Red
MAIN SET	4 x 400 IM (pink - red - blue - max for time)

WEEK 4	Wed Sep 20 2023
WARMUP	1 x 400 Free 1 x 300 Choice 2 x 200 Kick 3 x 100 IM 6 x 100 DPS @ :50

SPRINT	4 x 200 @ 3:00
	(2) White (1) Pink
	(1:00)
	4 x 100 Pink – Red – Blue- MAX @ 1:20
	2 x {
	   8 x 50 @ :50
	   (:30)
	   4 x 25 underwater @ :40
	}

DISTANCE	10 x (50+50 easy) 500 – Hold 500 Goal pace –2 200 – Hold 200 Goal pace – 1 5 x (100 + 100 easy) 500 – Hold 500 Goal Pace 200 – Hold 200 goal pace +1 3 x (200 + 100 easy) D 1-3
MID-DISTANCE	12 x 75 (2 easy @ 1:10, 1 FAST @ 1:00) 1 x 600 Pull @ 7:00/7:50 4 x 75 Kick @ 1:20 odds: White-Pink-Red Evens: Red-Pink-White (1:00) 1 x 600 Pull @ 6:50/7:40 4 x 100 Kick @ 1:30/1:40 Descend to MAX start @ Pink (2:00) 2 x 500 Swim @ 5:20/5:40 (2:00) 4 x 200 Swim w/fins @ 2:15

WEEK 3	Thu Sep 21 2023
WARMUP	4 x 200 @ :15 rest odds: Free evens: (50 back drill/50 Choice) 10 x 25 Build each 25 to fast flip @ :50 8 x 25 (12.5 underwater kick sprint/12.5 breakout MAX, easy) @ :30 8 x 50 w/fins (12.5 underwater Kick Red/12.5 Swim no breath/25 white) @ 1:00 (1:00) 8 x 25 @ :40 odds: Build evens: Accelerate
MAIN SET	5 x 100 Negative Split (50 White/50 Blue) @ 1:20 Stroke - Free White/Stroke Blue (1:00) 5 x 100 MAX Kick @ 2:00 (3:00) 5 x 100 D1-5 to MAX @ 1:20 All Stroke (1:00) 5 x 50 MAX Kick @ 1:20 (3:00)

WEEK 4	Fri Sep 22 2023
WARMUP	4 x 200 #1 Free #2 Back/Breast by 50's #3 100 BK/100 Choice #4 Free 1 x 300 Kick 2 x 200 (100 White/100 Red Kick @ 3:30 6 x 50 D1-3 to Pink, 4-6 to MAX (start at White) @ 1:00 6 x 100 Paddle w/Pull Buoy @ 1:20/1:30 6 x 75 Descend @ 1:10 odds: fly-back-breast evens: back-breast-free
SPRINT	400 Free 200 Kick 100 IM 8 x 25 MAX on 1:00 10 x 25 w/ chutes @ :45 Red 10 x 25 x/ fins MAX underwater kick @ :30
DISTANCE	4 x (200 pull + 100 easy) Descend 7 x (100 + 50 easy) #1-5 Goal 500 Pace #6-7 Hold #5 Time 4 x (50 + 50 easy) All Fast
MID-DISTANCE	2 x 400 Paddle w/Pull Buoy @ 4:45/5:00 3 x 200 IM :30 sec 4 x 50 Free @ :40 2 x 300 (150 Free/150 Non-Free) @ 4 x 100 Descend @ 1:30 4 x 50 Free @ :40 4 x 25s Max start + breakout

WEEK 3	Sat Sep 23 2023
WARMUP	1 x 600 (300 Free / 200 Kick / 100 Breast)
	1 x 500 Kick
	1 x 400 Kick
	4 x 100 Kick (50 pink / 50 red) @ 1:50
	4 x 50 MAX Kick @ 1:00
	1 x 200 easy
MAIN SET	8 x 100 Build
	#1-4 w / fins @ 1:15 / 1:25
	#5-8 IM @ 1:30 / 1:40
	6 x 200 @ 2:55 / 3:10
	Descend 1-3 Blue
	6 x 100 @ 1:20 / 1:30
	Descend 1-3
	Ascend 4-6
	4 x 100 Kick Red @ 1:30

SEPTEMBER — ELITE SWIM WORKOUT '24 — WEEK 5

Monday

1 x 400 Free
1 x 300 Non-Free
1 x 200 Kick
1 x 100 IM

3 x 200 (200 Free/200 BK/200 BR)
1 x 400 (200 Kick/100 Free/100 Choice)
1 x 400 Paddle w/Pull Buoy DPS

SPRINT

4 x {
1 x 75 MAX
.30 rest
50 MAX from push
}

1 x 300 white
2 x 200 @ 2:30
White-Pink
8 x 25 w/fins Underwater @ :40

DISTANCE

4 x 200 @ 2:40, 2:50
Descend Each 200 + 25 Blue (1:00)
8 x 75 @ :50/:55FR, 1:00/1:10BK & BR (2:00)
4 x 200 @ 2:30/2:40 FR, 2:40/2:50BK, 2:50/3:00BR
#1-2 Negative Split
#3-4 Best time + 12 (2:00)
5 x 100 JMI @ 1:00/1:05/1:10

MID-DISTANCE

600 (300 White Free/300 Pink Back) @ 9:00
4 x 200 IM @ 2:40/2:45(1:00)
2 x 400 Fin Swim @ :20 rest
odds: BP: 5
evens: BP: 4
6 x 50 under/over w/fins @ 1:00
5 x 100 JMI @ 1:15
odds: (50 Free/50 Non-Free)
evens: Free

Tuesday

600 Free
6 x 100 IM D1-3 and 4-6 @ 1:30
10 x 100 (25 drill/50 swim/25 drill) @ 1:30

3 x { w/fins
25 underwater kick @ :30
50 Fly descend @ :40
75 Fast Kick - Flutter @ 1:00/1:10
100 FAST @ 2:00
}

2 x 400 IM JMI @ 4:30
4 x 50 Kick IMO @ :50 (1:00)
3 x 200 IM JMI @ 2:15
4 x 50 Kick IMO @ :50

Wednesday

6 x 150
odds: (Free/Non-Free/Free) by 50's
evens: (100 Kick/50 Breast)

3 x 600 @ +:15 rest
#1 Paddle/Pull
#2 Paddle
#3 Descend each 100 to Pink

SPRINT

6 x 75 Build @ 1:15
1 x 400 pull @ 5:00
5 x 100 (3) White (2) Pink @ 1:30
1 x 300 (150 Kick no board/ 150 Swim) @ 5:30
5 x 100 (3) White (1) Pink (1) Red @ 1:30

Cooldown

DISTANCE

1 x 300 w/fins
2 x 200 @ 2:30
#1 Build each 25 to Max FLIP
#2 Build each 50 to Pink

2 x {
4 x 100 Neg Split @ 1:30 (White/Pink)
4 x 50 Descend
4 x 25 Build
4 x 150 (breast/free/choice)
}

MID-DISTANCE

4 x {1-White, 2-Pink, 3-Red, 4-Blue
1 x (500 + 100 easy)
4 x (50 + 50) MAX
}

Thursday

1 x 600 Free
2 x 400 (200 Kick/200 Back)
4 x 100
odds: IM
evens: (50 Breast Kick/50 Swim)

10 x 50 (Kick/Drill) @ :55
1 x 400 Paddle/Fins
4 x 25 sprint kick @ :50

3 x 400 w/fins BP: 3,5 by 100s @ 5:10
3 x 100 w/fins @ 1:15

2 x {
3 x 200 Paddle w/Pull Buoy
6 x 100 @ 1:05/1:10
}

Friday

4 x 200 @ :15 rest
odds: IMO
evens: (50 free drill/50 Choice)

1 x 300 (150 Kick no board/ 150 Swim) @ 5:30
1 x 500 white
2 x 300 Pull @ 3:45/4:00
10 x 50 @ 1:00
Odds 50 Free
Evens 50 Non Free

SPRINT

12 x 50 (2 white @ 1:00, 1 red @ 1:00)
1 x 200 Pull @ 3:00
4 x 50 Kick @ 1:00
odds: White-Pink-Red
Evens: Red-Pink-White (1:00)

1 x 400 Pull @ 5:00
4 x 100 Kick @ 1:40
Descend to MAX start @ Pink (2:00)
2 x 200 Swim @ 2:30 (2:00)
2x 200 Kick w/fins @ 2:20/2:30

DISTANCE

3 x 100 (white/pink/red) @ 1:40
2 x 100 Pink – Red @ 1:30
4 x 50 D 1-4 @ 1:10

25's from a dive MAX
6 x 25 build to max finish
4 x 200 (free/stroke/kick) @ 3:00

MID-DISTANCE

4 x 400 D 1-4 @ 4:40/5:00
1 x 800 Strong @ 9:30/10:00
8 x 100 @ 1:05/1:10

Saturday

3 x 400
#1 (200 Free/200 Back) @ :20 rest
#2 (200 Kick/200 Free) @ :20 rest
#3 (200 Choice/200 Kick no board)

4 x 50 choice @ 1:10

3 x 300 (100 Moderate/100 Drill/100 Build to Pink) @ 3:50/4:00/4:10
4 x 100 Negative Split (50 White/50 Red) @ 1:10/1:20
4 x 50 @ :40

6 x 200 @ 3:00 (White-Pink x 3)
5 x 100 JMI @ 1:10/1:15
4 x 200 (100 White/100 Build) @ 2:40 (1:00)
4 x 100 @ 1:40
4 x 100 Descend @ 1:20/1:30

WEEK 5	Mon Sep 25 2023
WARMUP	1 x 400 Free 1 x 300 Non-Free 1 x 200 Kick 1 x 100 IM 3 x 200 (200 Free/200 BK/200 BR) 1 x 400 (200 Kick/100 Free/100 Choice) 1 x 400 Paddle w/Pull Buoy DPS

SPRINT	4 x {
	   1 x 75 MAX
	   :30 rest
	   50 MAX from push
	}
	1 x 300 white
	2 x 200 @ 2:30
	White-Pink
	8 x 25 w/fins Underwater @ :40

DISTANCE	4 x 200 @ 2:40, 2:50 Descend Each 200 + 25 Blue (1:00) 8 x 75 @ :50/:55FR, 1:00/1:10BK & BR (2:00) 4 x 200 @ 2:30/2:40 FR, 2:40/2:50BK, 2:50/3:00BR #1-2 Negative Split #3-4 Best time + 12 (2:00) 5 x 100 JMI @ 1:00/1:05/1:10
MID-DISTANCE	600 (300 White Free/300 Pink Back) @ 9:00 4 x 200 IM @ 2:40/2:45(1:00) 2 x 400 Fin Swim @ :20 rest odds: BP: 5 evens: BP: 4 6 x 50 under/over w/fins @ 1:00 5 x 100 JMI @ 1:15 odds: (50 Free/50 Non-Free) evens: Free

WEEK 5	Tue Sep 26 2023

WARMUP	600 Free
	6 x 100 IM D1-3 and 4-6 @ 1:30
	
	10 x 100 (25 drill/50 swim/25 drill) @ 1:30
	
	3 x { w/fins
	  25 underwater kick @ :30
	  50 Fly descend @ :40
	  75 Fast Kick - Flutter @ 1:00/1:10
	  100 FAST @ 2:00
	  }

MAIN SET	2 x 400 IM JMI @ 4:30 4 x 50 Kick IMO @ :50 (1:00) 3 x 200 IM JMI @ 2:15 4 x 50 Kick IMO @ :50

WEEK 5	Wed Sep 27 2023
WARMUP	6 x 150 odds: (Free/Non-Free/Free) by 50's evens: (100 Kick/50 Breast) 3 x 600 @ + :15 rest #1 Paddle/Pull #2 Paddle #3 Descend each 100 to Pink
SPRINT	6 x 75 Build @ 1:15 1 x 400 pull @ 5:00 5 x 100 (3) White (2) Pink @ 1:30 1 x 300 (150 Kick no board / 150 Swim) @ 5:30 5 x 100 (3) White (1) Pink (1) Red @ 1:30 Cooldown

DISTANCE	1 x 300 w/fins
	2 x 200 @ 2:30
	#1 Build each 25 to Max FLIP
	#2 Build each 50 to Pink
	
	2 x {
	4 x 100 Neg Split @ 1:30
	(White/Pink)
	4 x 50 Descend
	4 x 25 Build
	4 x 150 (breast/free/choice)
	}

MID-DISTANCE	4 x { 1-White, 2-Pink, 3-Red, 4-Blue
	   1 x (500 + 100 easy)
	   4 x (50 + 50) MAX
	}

WEEK 5	Thu Sep 28 2023
WARMUP	1 x 600 Free 2 x 400 (200 Kick/200 Back) 4 x 100 odds: IM evens: (50 Breast Kick/50 Swim) 10 x 50 (Kick/Drill) @ :55 1 x 400 Paddle/Fins 4 x 25 sprint kick @ :50

MAIN SET	3 x 400 w/fins BP: 3,5 by 100s @ 5:10
	3 x 100 w/fins @ 1:15
	
	2 x {
	   3 x 200 Paddle w/Pull Buoy
	   6 x 100 @ 1:05/1:10
	}

WEEK 5	Fri Sep 29 2023
WARMUP	4 x 200 @ :15 rest odds: IMO evens: (50 free drill/50 Choice) 1 x 300 (150 Kick no board / 150 Swim) @ 5:30 1 x 500 white 2 x 300 Pull @ 3:45/4:00 10 x 50 @ 1:00 Odds 50 Free Evens 50 Non Free
SPRINT	12 x 50 (2 white @ 1:00, 1 red @ 1:00) 1 x 200 Pull @ 3:00 4 x 50 Kick @ 1:00 odds: White-Pink-Red Evens: Red-Pink-White (1:00) 1 x 400 Pull @ 5:00 4 x 100 Kick @ 1:40 Descend to MAX start @ Pink (2:00) 2 x 200 Swim @ 2:30 (2:00) 2x 200 Kick w/fins @ 2:20/2:30
DISTANCE	3 x 100 (white/pink/red) @ 1:40 2 x 100 Pink – Red @ 1:30 4 x 50 D 1-4 @ 1:10 25's from a dive MAX 6 x 25 build to max finish 4 x 200 (free/stroke/kick) @ 3:00
MID-DISTANCE	4 x 400 D 1-4 @ 4:40/5:00 1 x 800 Strong @ 9:30/10:00 8 x 100 @ 1:05/1:10

WEEK 5	Sat Sep 30 2023
WARMUP	3 x 400 #1 (200 Free/200 Back) @ :20 rest #2 (200 Kick/200 Free) @ :20 rest #3 (200 Choice/200 Kick no board) 4 x 50 choice @ 1:10
MAIN SET	3 x 300 (100 Moderate/100 Drill/100 Build to Pink) @ 3:50/4:00/4:10 4 x 100 Negative Split (50 White/50 Red) @ 1:10/1:20 4 x 50 @ :40 6 x 200 @ 3:00 (White-Pink x 3) 5 x 100 JMI @ 1:10/1:15 4 x 200 (100 White/100 Build) @ 2:40 (1:00) 4 x 100 @ 1:40 4 x 100 Descend @ 1:20/1:30

OCTOBER   ELITE SWIM WORKOUT '24   WEEK 6

Monday	Tuesday	Wednesday	Thursday	Friday	Saturday

200 SKIMPS
8 x 50 IMO @ :50
300 White
 	
6 x 75 w/fins (25 underwater kick/25 swim/25 underwater kick) @ 1:20 (1:00)
 	
3 x 200 Free @ 2:30 D 1-3
4 x (100 Fast + 50 easy)
 	
SPRINT
5 x 75 Red @ 3:00
6 x 50 Blue@ 2:00
 	
400 IM
4 x 100 @ 1:30
odds: Free evens: Non-free
5 x 50 drill @ 1:00
8 x 50 @ 1:00
 	
DISTANCE
2 x 500 @ 6:30/7:00/7:20
#1 Build each 50 to Pink
#2 3Descend each 100 starting at Pink
 	
6 x 200
#1-2 IM @ 2:30/2:40/2:50
#3-4 Swim @ 2:20/2:30
#5-6 RIMO (drill fly) @ 2:30/2:40/2:50
 	
2 x {
1 x 300 @ 3:30/3:40/3:50
4 x 50 @ :40
}
MID-DISTANCE
1 x 600 Paddles/Pull
Bp 3-5 by 100s
1 x 400 Build
 	
10 x 100 JMI @ 1:10/1:15
Keep all the same speed
 	
3 x (100 + 100 easy)
Hold 1000 Pace
	1 x 500 White Kick
	Non-Stop{
	400 Kick-400 Pull-400 Swim
	300 Kick-300 Pull-300 Swim
	200 Kick- 200 Pull- 200 Swim
	100 Kick- 100 Pull- 100 Swim
	}
	
	6 x 50 Fingertip drill @ 1:00
	4 x 100 Catch-up drill @ 2:00
	2 x 100 Fly Kick
	
	SPRINT
	3 X {
	4 x 100 @ 1:30
	#1: 25 max, 75 Pink
	#2: 25 pink, 25 max, 50 Pink
	#3: 50 pink, 25 max, 25 Pink
	#4: 75 pink, 25 max
	30 sec rest
	}
	1 x 200
	alt 50 scull, 50 kick
		1 x 100 SKIMPS
		
		4 x 50 kick no board #1 stroke @ :50
		
		2 x {
		3 x 50 fist drill @ 1:00
		8 x 25 #1 Stroke drill @ :45
		fly: press/pop, back catchup, Breast pull w/ little paddles, Free: single arm
		4 x 25 build @ :30
		}
		4 x 100 (50 #1 Stroke/50 Free) @ 1:30
		
		SPRINT
		6 x 12.5 MAX
		2 x (300 + 100 white)
		#1 Work Turns & MAX Breakout
		#2 Great Finish MAX @ every wall (1:00)
		4 x (100 + 50 white)
		(2) White (2) Pink
		8 x (50 + 50 white)
		#1-4 200 Best Time
		#5-8 Hold Goal 200 Pace -1
		
		DISTANCE
		4 x 200 @ + :20
		#1 Free #2 Non-Free #3 BK/Kick by 50's #4 IM (1:00)
		12 x 50
		#1-6 Neg Split (Clear/Pink) @ :45
		#7-12 No Breath off walls for 3 Strokes @ :45
		
		4 x 100 @ + :10
		#1 Free #2 Past flags on each wall choice #3 Non-Free #4 Drill
		(1:00)
		6 x 100
		#1-3 D1-3
		#4-6 Fast breakout on each wall
		8 x 50 w/fins (25 underwater/25 swim) @ 1:10
		
		2 x 400 Fin Swim
		#1 Free
		#2 IM
		
		MID-DISTANCE
		1 x 1000 Broken
		(10 x 100 @ :20 rest)
		1 x 1500 Broken
		(10 x 50 @ :10 rest)
		4 x 75 Paddle w/Pull Buoy
			500 Choice
			200 Kick
			200 IM
			
			12 x 75 @
			#1-4 (50 Free/25 BK)
			#5-8 (25 Kick no board/50 Breast)
			#9-12 (Fly/Back/Breast)
			
			4 x 200 Paddle/Pull
			
			8 x 50 @ :50
			
			IM
			3 x 300 IMO @ 4:10/4:204 x 50 BR Pull @ :55/1:00
			3 x 150 (100 BR/50 BACK) @ 2:20/2:10
			4 x 50 back Pull @ :50/:55
			4 x 75 (50 Back/25 Fly) @ 1:00/1:05
			4 x 50 Fly Pull @ :50/:55
				4 x 100 Freestyle
				3 x 100 Fly
				2 x 100 Back
				1 x 100 Breast
				
				10 x 25 Build each 25 to fast flip @ 1:10
				8 x 25 (12.5 underwater kick sprint/12.5 breakout MAX, easy) @ :30
				
				1 x 200 Choice
				6 x 50 Paddle @ :50
				
				SPRINT
				4 x 100 feet past flags on every wall @ 1:30
				8 x 25 Sprints @ :30
				
				2 x 400 #1 Free #2Back/Breast by 50's
				4 x 125 Paddle/fins working on awesome catch @ 1:30
				300 Non Free
				4 x 100 @ 1:20/1:30 MAX
				300 Cooldown
				
				DISTANCE
				5 x {
				400 @ 4:45/4:50
				4 x 100 Goal 500 Pace -1 @ 1:10/1:15/1:20
				1:00 rest
				}
				
				MID-DISTANCE
				4 x 200
				Pull/Kick/Pink/White
				2 x 800
				odd 100s: Descend
				even 100s Kick Pink
				6 x 200
				odds: Blue @ 2:20
				evens: IM @ 2:40
				5 x 100s
				(100s Descend 1-5 Red)
					3 x 200 - #1 Free #2 Non-Free #3 Choice
					4 x 100 IM White
					
					3 x 400
					#1 Paddle w/Pull Buoy @ 5:00/5:10/5:20
					#2 Swim BP: 3.5 by 100 @ 4:40/4:50/5:00
					#3 Swim (75 Free/25 Back w/1/2 underwater kick)
					
					1 x 300 Free @ 4:30
					2 x 200 Descend @ 3:00
					3 x 100 Descend @ 1:30
					4 x 50 max @ 1:30
					
					1 x 400 cool down

WEEK 6	Mon Oct 02 2023
WARMUP	200 SKIMPS 8 x 50 IMO @ :50 300 White 6 x 75 w/fins (25 underwater kick/25 swim/25 underwater kick) @ 1:20 (1:00) 3 x 200 Free @ 2:30 D 1-3 4 x (100 Fast + 50 easy)
SPRINT	5 x 75 Red @ 3:00 6 x 50 Blue@ 2:00 400 IM 4 x 100 @ 1:30 odds: Free evens: Non-free 5 x 50 drill @ 1:00 8 x 50 @ 1:00

DISTANCE	2 x 500 @ 6:30/7:00/7:20
	#1 Build each 50 to Pink
	#2 3Descend each 100 starting at Pink
	
	6 x 200
	#1-2 IM @ 2:30/2:40/2:50
	#3-4 Swim @ 2:20/2:30
	#5-6 RIMO (drill fly) @ 2:30/2:40/2:50
	
	2 x {
	  1 x 300 @ 3:30/3:40/3:50
	  4 x 50 @ :40
	}

MID-DISTANCE	1 x 600 Paddle/Pull Bp 3-5 by 100s 1 x 400 Build 10 x 100 JMI @ 1:10/1:15 Keep all the same speed 3 x (100 + 100 easy) Hold 1000 Pace

WEEK 6	Tue Oct 03 2023

WARMUP	1 x 500 White Kick
	Non-Stop{
	   400 Kick-400 Pull-400 Swim
	   300 Kick-300 Pull-300 Swim
	   200 Kick- 200 Pull- 200 Swim
	   100 Kick- 100 Pull- 100 Swim
	}
	
	6 x 50 Fingertip drill @ 1:00
	4 x 100 Catch-up drill @ 2:00
	2 x 100 Fly Kick

MAIN SET	3 X {
	   4 x 100 @ 1:30
	   #1: 25 max, 75 Pink
	   #2: 25 pink, 25 max, 50 Pink
	   #3: 50 pink, 25 max, 25 Pink
	   #4: 75 pink, 25 max
	
	   30 sec rest
	}
	1 x 200
	alt 50 scull, 50 kick

WEEK 6	Wed Oct 04 2023

WARMUP	1 x 100 SKIMPS
	4 x 50 kick no board #1 stroke @ :50
	2 x {
	   3 x 50 fist drill @ 1:00
	   8 x 25 #1 Stroke drill @ :45
	   fly: press/pop, back: catchup, Breast: pull w/ little paddles, Free: single arm
	   4 x 25 build @ :30
	}
	4 x 100 (50 #1 Stroke/50 Free) @ 1:30

SPRINT	6 x 12.5 MAX 2 x (300 + 100 white) #1 Work Turns & MAX Breakout #2 Great Finish MAX @ every wall (1:00) 4 x (100 + 50 white) (2) White (2) Pink 8 x (50 + 50 white) #1-4 200 Best Time #5-8 Hold Goal 200 Pace –1
DISTANCE	4 x 200 @ + :20 #1 Free #2 Non-Free #3 BK/Kick by 50's #4 IM (1:00) 12 x 50 #1-6 Neg Split (Clear/Pink) @ :45 #7-12 No Breath off walls for 3 Strokes @ :45 4 x 100 @ + :10 #1 Free #2 Past flags on each wall choice #3 Non-Free #4 Drill (1:00) 6 x 100 #1-3 D1-3 #4-6 Fast breakout on each wall 8 x 50 w/fins (25 underwater/25 swim) @ 1:10 2 x 400 Fin Swim #1 Free #2 IM
MID-DISTANCE	1 x 1000 Broken (10 x 100 @ :20 rest) 1 x 500 Broken (10 x 50 @ :10 rest) 4x 75 Paddle w/Pull Buoy

WEEK 6	Thu Oct 05 2023
WARMUP	500 Choice 200 Kick 200 IM 12 x 75 @ #1-4 (50 Free/25 BK) #5-8 (25 Kick no board/50 Breast) #9-12 (Fly/Back/Breast) 4 x 200 Paddle/Pull 8 x 50 @ :50
MAIN SET	3 x 300 IMO @ 4:10/4:204 x 50 BR Pull @ :55/1:00 3 x 150 (100 BR/50 BACK) @ 2:20/2:10 4 x 50 back Pull @ :50/:55 4 x 75 (50 Back/25 Fly) @ 1:00/1:05 4 x 50 Fly Pull @ :50/:55

WEEK 6	Fri Oct 06 2023
WARMUP	4 x 100 Freestyle 3 x 100 Fly 2 x 100 Back 1 x 100 Breast 10 x 25 Build each 25 to fast flip @ 1:10 8 x 25 (12.5 underwater kick sprint/12.5 breakout MAX, easy) @ :30 1 x 200 Choice 6 x 50 Paddle @ :50
SPRINT	4 x 100 feet past flags on every wall @ 1:30 8 x 25 Sprints @ :30 2 x 400 #1 Free #2Back/Breast by 50's 4 x 125 Paddle/fins working on awesome catch @ 1:30 (1:00) 300 Non Free 4 x 100 @ 1:20/1:30 MAX 300 Cooldown

DISTANCE	5 x {
	   400 @ 4:45/4:50
	   4 x 100 Goal 500 Pace –1 @ 1:10/1:15/1:20
	   1:00 rest
	}

MID-DISTANCE	4 x 200 Pull/Kick/Pink/White 2 x 800 odd 100s: Descend even 100s Kick Pink 6 x 200 odds: Blue @ 2:20 evens: IM @ 2:40 5 x 100s (100s Descend 1-5 Red)

WEEK 6	Sat Oct 07 2023
WARMUP	3 x 200 - #1 Free #2 Non-Free #3 Choice 4 x 100 IM White 3 x 400 #1 Paddle w/Pull Buoy @ 5:00/5:10/5:20 #2 Swim BP: 3,5 by 100 @ 4:40/4:50/5:00 #3 Swim (75 Free/25 Back w/1/2 underwater kick)
MAIN SET	1 x 300 Free @ 4:30 2 x 200 Descend @ 3:00 3 x 100 Descend @ 1:30 4 x 50 max @ 1:30 1 x 400 cool down

OCTOBER — ELITE SWIM WORKOUT '24 — WEEK 7

Monday

400 IM
6 x 100 Kick w/Board
4 x 100 IM Order @ :15 rest

1 x 600 Paddle/Pull
Bp 5 by 100's work on great turns
1 x 400
SPRINT
4 x 200 @ 2:40
1 white, 2 pink, 1 red
10 x 100 @ 1:25
4 white, 3 pink, 3 red
12 x 50 @ :50
6 pink, 6 red
1 x 200 Kick white @ 4:00
6 x 50 kick @ 1:00
D 1-3, 4-6
DISTANCE
3 x 400 @ 4:50/5:00
Descend
3 x 200 @ 2:20/2:30
3 x 300 @ 3:30/3:45
Descend
4 x 50 Easy @ 1:00
MID-DISTANCE
1 x (600 Pink + 200 easy)
Descend
4 x (300 + 100)
Descend
(1:00)
8 x (100 Red+ 100 easy)
(1:00)
4 x 200 All Red
(1:00)
8 x (50 + 50 easy)
Hold 1000 Goal Pace

Tuesday

1 x 500 (250 Free/200 Non-Free/50 BK)
1 x 400 (200 Kick/200 Kick no board)
1 x 200 RIMO

6 x 50 (25 fist/25 pink) @ 1:00
Concentrate on high elbow catch
6 x 50 Free Underwater Recovery Drill @ 1:00
1 x 400
SPRINT
1 x 400 Kick w/fins
5 x 50 Kick w/fins dolphin on back @ :50
6 x 25 underwater MAX kick w/fins @ :25

6 x 100 JMI @ 1:20/1:30
odds: #1 Stroke
evens: IM
2 x (4 x 25 IMO Blue no breath on Fly/Free) @ :30
(2:00)
4 x {
100 IM w/chute @ 1:40/150
75 Fly Descend @ 1:10/1:15
50 Back (25 kick underwater/25 swim) @ :50/:55
25 Breast DPS w/ MAX kick @ :30
50 Free MAX @ 3:00
}

Wednesday

6 x 150
odds: Free
evens: Choice

4 x 100 IM @ 2:00
RB2 on last 25 Free

5 x 50 @ 1:00
5 x 50 drill same stroke different drill @ 1:00
12 x 50 Paddle/Pull @ :45
SPRINT
4 x 200 @ 2:30/2:40
(2) White-Pink-Red
4 x 100 JMI @ 1:10/120
(1:00)
8 x 50 Hold Goal 200 Pace + 1 @ 1:00
4 x 150 JMI @ 1:10/120
(2:00)
6 x 50 @ 1:00
DPS max of BR: 5 @ 1:10
DISTANCE
1 x 600 Kick (300 Kick No board/300 Kick Board)
6 x 50 Kick @ 1:00
#1-3 Worst Stroke
#4-6 Best Stroke
4 x 200 @ 4:50/5:00
White-Pink-White-Pink
2 x 200 IM @ 2:45/3:00
2 x 200's MAX @ 2:30
2 x 100's MAX @ 1:30
4 x 50's MAX @ :50
4 x 25's MAX @ :30
MID-DISTANCE
4 x 200 choice @ 2:40/2:50
(1:00)
4 x 150 (50 White/100 build) @ 1:50/2:00
20 x 100 Maintain best average @ 1:20/1:30

1 x 400 Free easy
5 x 100 Kick MAX @ 2:00

Thursday

1 x 300 Free
1 x 200 Non-Free
1 x 100 Kick
4 x 50 IMO @ :10 rest
6 x 150 w/fins @ :10
odd: kick-swim-kick
even: swim-kick-swim
2 x {
6 x 50 Kick w/fins @ :40
4 x 25 Underwater w/fins @ :30
(1:00)
}
2 x 400 IM@ 4:50/5:10
(1:00)
2 x 200 IM @ 2:20/2:30
Pink-Red
10 x 100 IM
odds: Blue @ 1:30
evens: Pink@ 1:50
12 x 50 all FAST @ 1:00

Friday

4 x 100 Freestyle
2 x {
4 x 50 fist drill @ 1:00
4 x 25 build @ :30
}
8 x 50 Kick @ 1:00
D1-4 , 5-8 to MAX (start at Pink)
SPRINT
4 x kick w/fins underwater
2 x 200 White @ 3:00
100 @ 1:20/1:30
(2) @ 1:10 or faster
(2) @ 1:08 or faster
(2) @ 1:05 or faster
(1) @ 1:02 or faster
(1) @ 1:00 or faster
(1) @ :59 or faster
(1) @ :58 or faster
(1) @ :57 or faster
(1) @ :56 or faster
(1) @ :54 or faster
(1) @ :52
(1) @ :50
DISTANCE
1 x 400 (100 Free/100 Back)
2 x 200 Stroke @ 2:45
Pink – Red
4 x 50 (12.5 underwater MAX kick + MAX breakout/12.5 easy swim) @ 1:00
2 x {
1 x 25 MAX from Dive @ :35/:40
1 x 75 JMI @ 1:15
1 x 50 kick ½ way underwater on every wall @ :40/:45
1 x 25 MAX underwater kick from Dive @ :40
1 x 100 MAX for time
}
6 x 100 @ 1:40
MID-DISTANCE
8 x 75 (drill/swim/drill) @ 1:15
8 x 50 Kick D 1-4 , 5-8 to MAX @ 1:00
4 x 300 White @ 3:50/4:00
4 x 250 White @ 3:00/3:30
4 x 200 Pink @ 2:30/2:40/2:50
4 x 100 Red @ 1:10/1:15/1:20
8 x 50 @ :40 JMI

Saturday

1 x 400 IM
3 x 100 Freestyle
2 x 200 IM

4 x 100 IMO (Kick/Drill/Swim/Drill) @ 2:20
3 x 200 Free
4 x 25 kick red @ :30

4 x 100 IM @ 1:35
4 x 50 Fast Kick @ 1:10
1 x 200 white
10 x 100 MAX Kick @ 1:50
500 Cooldown

WEEK 7	Mon Oct 09 2023
WARMUP	400 IM 6 x 100 Kick w/Board 4 x 100 IM Order @ :15 rest 1 x 600 Paddle/Pull Bp 5 by 100's work on great turns 1 x 400
SPRINT	4 x 200 @ 2:40 1 white, 2 pink, 1 red 10 x 100 @ 1:25 4 white, 3 pink, 3 red 12 x 50 @ :50 6 pink, 6 red 1 x 200 Kick white @ 4:00 6 x 50 kick @ 1:00 D 1-3, 4-6
DISTANCE	3 x 400 @ 4:50/5:00 Descend 4 x 50 Easy @ 1:00 3 x 300 @ 3:30/3:45 Descend 4 x 50 Easy @ 1:00 3 x 200 @ 2:20/2:30 Descend 4 x 50 Easy @ 1:00
MID-DISTANCE	1 x (600 Pink + 200 easy) 4 x (300 + 100) Descend (1:00) 8 x (100 Red+ 100 easy) (1:00) 4 x 200 All Red (1:00) 8 x (50 + 50 easy) Hold 1000 Goal Pace

WEEK 7	Tue Oct 10 2023
WARMUP	1 x 500 (250 Free/200 Non-Free/50 BK) 1 x 400 (200 Kick/200 Kick no board) 1 x 200 RIMO 6 x 50 (25 fist/25 pink) @ 1:00 Concentrate on high elbow catch 6 x 50 Free Underwater Recovery Drill @ 1:00 1 x 400 Kick w/fins 5 x 50 Kick w/fins dolphin on back @ :50 6 x 25 underwater MAX kick w/fins @ :25

MAIN SET	6 x 100 JMI @ 1:20/1:30
	odds: #1 Stroke
	evens: IM
	2 x (4 x 25 IMO Blue no breath on Fly/Free) @ :30
	(2:00)
	
	4 x {
	   100 IM w/chute @ 1:40/1:50
	   75 Fly Descend @ 1:10/1:15
	   50 Back (25 kick underwater/25 swim) @ :50/:55
	   25 Breast DPS w/ MAX kick @ :30
	   50 Free MAX @ 3:00
	}

WEEK 7	Wed Oct 11 2023
WARMUP	6 x 150 odds: Free evens: Choice 4 x 100 IM @ 2:00 RB:2 on last 25 Free 5 x 50 @ 1:00 5 x 50 drill same Stroke different drill @ 1:00 12 x 50 Paddle/Pull @ :45
SPRINT	4 x 200 @ 2:30/2:40 (2) White-Pink-Red 4 x 100 JMI @ 1:10/1:20 (1:00) 8 x 50 Hold Goal 200 Pace + 1 @ 1:00 4 x 100 JMI @ 1:10/1:20 (2:00) 6 x 50 @ 1:00 DPS max of BR: 5 @ 1:10
DISTANCE	1 x 600 Kick (300 Kick No board/300 Kick Board) 6 x 50 Kick @ 1:00 #1-3 Worst Stroke #4-6 Best Stroke 4 x 200 @ 4:50/5:00 White-Pink-White-Pink 2 x 200 IM @ 2:45/3:00 2 x 200's MAX @ 2:30 2 x 100's MAX @ 1:30 4 x 50's MAX @ :50 4 x 25's MAX @ :30
MID-DISTANCE	4 x 200 choice @ 2:40/2:50 (1:00) 4 x 150 (50 White/100 build) @ 1:50/2:00 20 x 100 Maintain best average@ 1:20/1:30 1 x 400 Free easy 5 x 100 Kick MAX @ 2:00

WEEK 7	Thu Oct 12 2023

WARMUP	1 x 300 Free
	1 x 200 Non-Free
	1 x 100 Kick
	4 x 50 IMO @ :10 rest
	6 x 150 w/fins @ :10
	odd: kick-swim-kick
	even: swim-kick-swim
	
	2 x {
	   6 x 50 Kick w/fins @ :40
	   4 x 25 Underwater w/fins @ :30
	   (1:00)
	}

MAIN SET	2 x 400 IM@ 4:50/5:10 (1:00) 2 x 200 IM @ 2:20/2:30 Pink-Red 10 x 100 IM odds: Blue @ 1:30 evens: Pink@ 1:50 12 x 50 all FAST @ 1:00

WEEK 7	Fri Oct 13 2023

WARMUP	4 x 100 Freestyle
	2 x {
	    4 x 50 fist drill @ 1:00
	    4 x 25 build @ :30
	}
	8 x 50 Kick @ 1:00
	D1-4 , 5-8 to MAX (start at Pink)

SPRINT	4 x kick w/ fins underwater 2 x 200 White @ 3:00 100 @ 1:20/1:30 (2) @ 1:10 or faster (2) @ 1:08 or faster (2) @ 1:05 or faster (1) @ 1:02 or faster (1) @ 1:00 or faster (1) @ :59 or faster (1) @ :58 or faster (1) @ :57 or faster (1) @ :56 or faster (1) @ :54 or faster (1) @ :52 (1) @ :50

DISTANCE	1 x 400 (100 Free/100 Back)
	2 x 200 Stroke @ 2:45
	Pink – Red
	4 x 50 (12.5 underwater MAX kick + MAX breakout/12.5 easy swim) @ 1:00
	
	2 x {
	    1 x 25 MAX from Dive @ :35/:40
	    1 x 75 JMI @ 1:15
	    1 x 50 kick ½ way underwater on every wall @ :40/:45
	    1 x 25 MAX underwater kick from Dive @ :40
	    1 x 100 MAX for time
	}
	6 x 100 @ 1:40

MID-DISTANCE	8 x 75 (drill/swim/drill) @ 1:15 8 x 50 Kick D 1-4 , 5-8 to MAX @ 1:00 4 x 300 White @ 3:50/4;00 4 x 250 White @ 3:00/3:30 4 x 200 Pink @ 2:30/2:40/2:50 4 x 100 Red @ 1:10/1:15/1:20 8 x 50 @ :40 JMI

WEEK 7	Sat Oct 14 2023
WARMUP	1 x 400 IM 3 x 100 Freestyle 2 x 200 IM 4 x 100 IMO (Kick/Drill/Swim/Drill) @ 2:20 3 x 200 Free 4 x 25 kick red @ :30
MAIN SET	4 x 100 IM @ 1:35 4 x 50 Fast Kick @ 1:10 1 x 200 white 10 x 100 MAX Kick @ 1:50 500 Cooldown

Monday

1 x 200 Kick Breast
1 x 200 Kick Fly
1 x 200 Back
1 x 200 Kick Free

5 x 50 Dolphin on Back @ .50

12 x 75 Continuous IM @ 1:10
4 x 25 IMO Descend @ :30

SPRINT

4 x 25 MAX Breakout @ :30
4 x 50 no breath in or out of wall @ 1:10
2 x (10 x 50 @ 1:30) ALL OUT MAX

DISTANCE

6 x 25 @ :30
odds: MAX Breakout
evens: MAX finish

6 x (100 + 50 easy)
odds: Build each 25 to no breath in flags, fast finish
evens: max of 9 breaths

3 x 300 @ +-20
#1: Free-NonFree-Fee by 100
#2 BP: 3-5-3 by 100
#3 BP: 5-7 by 50

12 x 50 Choice @ 1:10
#1-4: Descend
#5-8: Descend
#9-12:Descend to Max
5 x 100 JMI @ 1:10/1:15/1:20

MID-DISTANCE

20 x 100 @ 1:30
#1-5 Negative Split(White/Red)
#6-20 Best Average

Tuesday

8 x 75 w/fins @ :55
Continuous IM (BR-dolphin kick), Work under waters - easy swim (:30)

4 x 50 IMO @ :50
25 underwater/25 swim (1:00)

3 x 300 Kick w/fins @ 3:45/4:00/4:10

DISTANCE

1 x 800 Paddle/Pull @ :20 rest
4 x 200 @ 2:50/3:00
White-Pink-Red-Blue

8 x 200 @ 2:20/2:30
#1 25 Blue/175 white
#2 50 Blue/150 white
etc...

Wednesday

2 x 400
#1 Free #2 IM by 100's

3 x 200
#1 RIMO #2 IM #3 Choice

10 x 75 continuous IM @ 1:10

SPRINT

12 x 100 IM @ 1:30

2 x {
4 x 50 Kick @ 1:00
1 x 200 IM @ 2:40
1 x 300 Negative Split (150 White/150 Red) @ 5:00
}

4 x 12.5 from the Block

DISTANCE

8 x 25 Sprints
1 x 300 Paddle w/Pull Buoy
10 x 100 JMI @ 1:05/1:20

2 x {
1 x 400 Stroke
4 x 50 @ 1:00
Descend 1-4
}
5 x 200 @ 2:30
1-3 all White, 4-5

6 x 50 Kick MAX @ 1:00

MID-DISTANCE

3 x 500 @ 7:45
Bp 5

4 x 400 Paddle/Pull D 1-4 @ 5:20

6 x 150 (fly/back/breast) w/ fins @ 2:10

6 x 150 @ 2:00
D 1-3, 4-6 to MAX

Thursday

200 Breast
200 Free
200 Kick
200 Back

16 x 50 @ .50
#1-4 sprint turns in & out of flags
#5-8 BK 15 yds underwater kick + fast breakout
#9-12 free with fast kick
#13-16 Fly 25 kick/25 fast

4 x 50 #1 drill, #2 build, #3 drill, #4 sprint @ :45
3 x 100 (white/pink/red) @ 1:40
2 x 100 Pink – Red @ 1:30
4 x 50 D 1-4 @ 1:15
6 x 25 build to max finish

Friday

300 FR
200 Kick
100 IM
1 x 500 Paddle/Pull

2 x {
1 x 400 Kick
4 x 50 Kick w/fins
}
4 x 100 @ 1:15/1:20
4 x 25 DPS @ :25 (:30)
4 x 100 Descend

SPRINT

5 x 100 MAX

DISTANCE

1 x 400 (200 White/200 Kick Red)
2 x 200 (100 Pink/100 Kick Red) @ 3:00/3:10
4 x 100 Descend to MAX @ 1:20/1:40

2 x {
2 x 100 JMI @ 1:40/1:50/2:00
2 x 75 Build each 25 to Pink @ 1:15/1:20/1:30
4 x 50 Red @ 1:05/1:10/1:15
8 x 25 @ 1:00
odds: from Dive
evens: from Push
}

MID-DISTANCE

3 x 200 Paddle/Pull
1 x 400 easy
8 x 200 @ 2:40
#1-2 Free
#3-4 (100 Kick/100 Swim)
#5-6 Non-Free
#7-8 RIMO
15 x 100 Free @ 1:30

Saturday

1 x 400 IM
4 x 200 IM @ 2:50
9 x 100 @ 1:15 BP: 3-5

10 x 50 @:50
Split by 25s
odds: RB 1 breath/ RB 2

5 x 100 (drill/swim) @ 1:40
2 x 200 #1 White #2 Pink @ 2:30
3 x 100 D1-3 to Pink @ 1:30
3 x 100 (drill/swim or kick/swim) @ 1:40

WEEK 8	Mon Oct 16 2023
WARMUP	1 x 200 Kick Breast 1 x 200 Kick Fly 1 x 200 Back 1 x 200 Kick Free 5 x 50 Dolphin on Back @ :50 12 x 75 Continuous IM @ 1:10 4 x 25 IMO Descend @ :30
SPRINT	4 x 25 MAX Breakout @ :30 4 x 50 no breath in or out of wall @ 1:10 2 x (10 x 50 @ 1:30) ALL OUT MAX
DISTANCE	3 x 400 @ 4:50/5:00 Descend 4 x 50 Easy @ 1:00 3 x 300 @ 3:30/3:45 Descend 4 x 50 Easy @ 1:00 3 x 200 @ 2:20/2:30 Descend 4 x 50 Easy @ 1:00
MID-DISTANCE	20 x 100 @ 1:30 #1-5 Negative Split(White/Red) #6-20 Best Average

WEEK 8	Tue Oct 17 2023

WARMUP	4 x 200 IM
	3 x 100 Freestyle
	1 x 200 Kick
	
	2 x {
	  x 50 fist drill @ 1:00
	  6 x 25 Build @ :30
	}
	
	    8 x 75 w/fins @ :55
	    Continuous IM (BR-dolphin kick), Work under waters - easy swim
	    (:30)
	    4 x 50 IMO @ :50
	    25 underwater/25 swim
	    (1:00)
	
	3 x 300 Kick w/fins @ 3:45/4:00/4:10

MAIN SET	1 x 800 Paddle/Pull @ :20 rest 4 x 200 @ 2:50/3:00 White-Pink-Red-Blue 8 x 200 @ 2:20/2:30 #1 25 Blue/175 white #2 50 Blue/150 white etc..

WEEK 8	Wed Oct 18 2023
WARMUP	2 x 400 #1 Free #2 IM by 100's 3 x 200 #1 RIMO #2 IM #3 Choice 10 x 75 continuous IM @ 1:10

SPRINT	12 x 100 IM @ 1:30
	2 x {
	   4 x 50 Kick @ 1:00
	   1 x 200 IM @ 2:40
	   1 x 300 Negative Split (150 White/150 Red) @ 5:00
	}
	
	4 x 12.5 from the Block

DISTANCE	8 x 25 Sprints
	1 x 300 Paddle w/Pull Buoy
	10 x 100 JMI @ 1:05/1:20
	
	2 x {
	   1 x 400 Stroke
	   4 x 50 @ 1:00
	   Descend 1-4
	}
	5 x 200 @ 2:30
	1-3 all White, 4-5
	
	6 x 50 Kick MAX @ 1:00

MID-DISTANCE	3 x 500 @ 7:45 Bp 5 4 x 400 Paddle/Pull D 1-4 @ 5:20 6 x 150 (fly/back/breast) w/ fins @ 2:10 6 x 150 @ 2:00 D 1-3, 4-6 to MAX

WEEK 8	Thu Oct 19 2023
WARMUP	200 Breast 200 Free 200 Kick 200 Back 16 x 50 @ :50 #1-4 sprint turns in & out of flags #5-8 BK 15 yds underwater kick + fast breakout #9-12 free with fast kick #13-16 Fly 25 kick/25 fast
MAIN SET	4 x 50 #1 drill, #2 build, #3 drill, #4 sprint @ :45 3 x 100 (white/pink/red) @ 1:40 2 x 100 Pink – Red @ 1:30 4 x 50 D 1-4 @ 1:15 6 x 25 build to max finish

WEEK 8	Fri Oct 20 2023

WARMUP	300 FR
	200 Kick
	100 IM
	1 x 500 Paddle/Pull
	
	2 x {
	   1 x 400 Kick
	   4 x 50 Kick w/fins
	}
	4 x 100 @ 1:15/1:20
	4 x 25 DPS @ :25
	(:30)
	4 x 100 Descend

SPRINT	5 x 100 MAX ALL OUT

DISTANCE	1 x 400 (200 White/200 Kick Red)
	2 x 200 (100 Pink/100 Kick Red) @ 3:00/3:10
	4 x 100 Descend to MAX @ 1:20/1:40
	
	2 x {
	   2 x 100 JMI @ 1:40/1:50/2:00
	   2 x 75 Build each 25 to Pink @ 1:15/1:20/1:30
	   4 x 50 Red @ 1:05/1:10/1:15
	   8 x 25 @ 1:00
	   odds: from Dive
	   evens: from Push
	}

MID-DISTANCE	3 x 200 Paddle/Pull 1 x 400 easy 8 x 200 @ 2:40 #1-2 Free #3-4 (100 Kick/100 Swim) #5-6 Non-Free #7-8 RIMO 15 x 100 Free @ 1:30

WEEK 8	Sat Oct 14 2023
WARMUP	1 x 400 IM 4 x 200 IM @ 2:50 9 x 100 @ 1:15 BP: 3-5 10 x 50 @:50 Split by 25s odds: RB 1 breath/ RB 2
MAIN SET	5 x 100 (drill/swim) @ 1:45 2 x 200 #1 White #2 Pink @ 2:40 3 x 100 D1-3 to Pink @ 1:30 3 x 100 (drill/swim or kick/swim) @ 1:40

OCTOBER — ELITE SWIM WORKOUT '24 — WEEK 9

Monday

3 x 300
#1 White/Pink @ 3:50/3:55
#2 (50 Pink/50 max of 4 breaths) @ 4:00
#3 No Breath in or out of walls

3 x (w/fins
25 underwater kick @ :30
50 Back descend @ :50
75 Fast Kick - Flutter @ 1:00/1:10
100 FAST @ 2:00
}

SPRINT
1 x 300 white
2 x {
100 Red from Blocks
200 white
100 MAX from push
100 white
}
2 x {
50 Red from Blocks
100 white
50 MAX from Push
50 white
}

DISTANCE
4 x 100 IM pink @ 1:50
1 x 200 Broken each 50 for :10 (1:00)
3 x 50 MAX from a dive @ 2:30 rest
4 x 25 MAX breakout @ :10 rest

4 x 100 White @ 4:00/4:10
4 x 100 Kick D1-4 @ 1:50
5 x 100 (25 kick BR/25 swim choice) @ 1:40

MID-DISTANCE
2 x (10 x100 @ 2:30) ALL OUT MAX

Tuesday

1 x 500 (250 Free/250 Back)
1 x 100 Scull on back, arms at side
1 x 100 Scull on front, arms at side

1 x 300 Scull
4 x 50 Dolphin on Back @ :50

4 x 100 (Kick/Drill) Worst Stroke @ 1:50
1 x 700 Paddle/Pull

4 x 100 IM @ 1:25
4 x 50 Fast Kick @ 1:00
1 x 200 white
10 x 100 MAX Kick @ 1:40
500 Cooldown

Wednesday

400 IM
8 x 50 Kick @ :10 rest
10 x 100 @ 15 rest
Odds: Fly
Evens: Free

3 x {
1 x 300 - Catchup Drill
5 x 50 drill - Choice @ 1:10
4 x 25 Stroke @ :40
}
10 x 50 w/fins 25 underwater kick/25 swim @ 1:00
4 x 25 underwater kick @ :40

SPRINT
1 x 200 (100 Red/100 Pink)
1 x 300 (100 White/100 Pink/100 Red)
(:30)
4 x 75 JMI @ :50/:55
2 x 200 (100 Pink/100 Red) @ 2:30 (1:00)
3 x 100 Best Average @ 2:00

DISTANCE
5 x 500's
(white - pink - red - blue - Max for time)

MID-DISTANCE
8 x 50 w/fins (12.5 underwater Kick Red/12.5 Swim no breath/25 easy) @ 1:00
8 x 25 @ :40
odds: Build
evens: Accelerate
8 x 100 Negative Split (50 White/50 Blue) @ 120FR/1:30 FR (1:00)
5 x 100 MAX Kick @ 2:00
8 x 100 @ 1:25/1:30
(2) Pink-(2) Red-(2) Blue- (2) MAX (1:00)
5 x 100 Pull Blue @ 1:30 (3:00)

Thursday

1 x 500 Free RB5
3 x 100 Kick
3 x 100 Free RB5

4 x 50 Descend Kick @ 1:00 (1:00)
8 x 50 Kick w/fins @ :40
1 x 300 Free Easy

4 x 200 @ 2:30/2:40
First 50 build to MAX turn + 3 Strokes breakout no breath (1:00)
4 x 100 @ 1:25/1:30
(25 no breath Red/75 Choice)

2 x 300 @ 3:40/3:50
#1 Negative Split - White/Pink
#2 Negative Split - White/Red

8 x 100 JMI
#1-4 @ 1:20/1:25
#5-8 @ 1:10/1:15

Friday

400 Kick
8 x 100 Choice @ 15 rest

8 x 25 w/fins FAST underwater kick @ :40
1 x 400 Kick White @ 7:00
4 x 50 (25 Blue/ 25 white) @ :50

SPRINT
15 x 100
#1-3 Free @ 1:30
#4-6 Build each 50 to MAX flip @ 1:30
#7-9 Kick @ 2:00
#10-12 (50 BK/50 Scull) @ 1:50
#13-15 D1-3 to Pink @ 1:30

400 Kick
4 x 50 Kick Descend

DISTANCE
6 x 25 (Drill/Build/Drill/Build/Drill/Sprint) @ :40
2x Broken 200's
(:20 secs each 100)
2 x Broken 100 (@ each 50 for :10 seconds)
1 x Broken 100 (@ each 25 for :10 seconds)

4 x 50 MAX @ :40
#1-2 max of 3 breaths
#3-4 max of 2 breaths

MID-DISTANCE
1 x 600 Paddle w/Pull Buoy
10 x 100 JMI @ 1:10/1:25
3 x {
1 x 75 Build @ 1:20
2 x 50 @ :50
1 x 500 Paddle w/Pull Buoy
2 x 200 @ 2:30/2:40
Pink-Red
}
2 x {
600 Choice
6 x 50 @ 1:00
White/Pink/Red/Blue/Max/Max
}

Saturday

400 RIMO
6 x 100 Non-Free (50 Kick/50 Swim) @ :10 rest

3 x 300 Paddle w/Pull Buoy @ 4:15 (:30)
3 x 100 Non-Free work walls @ 1:40

SPRINT
6 x 50 Fist Drill @ 1:00
6 x 25 Build @ :30

2 x 800 @ 10:00/11:00
White-Pink-Red-White by 100s
4 x 50 Kick Descend to MAX @ :55 (1:00)
2 x 500 @ 5:30/6:00
Pink- Red
4 x 50 Kick D1-4 at MAX @ 1:00 (2:00)
2 x 300 @ 3:30/3:45
Red-MAX
4 x 50 Kick Dolphin on back @ 1:00

WEEK 9	Mon Oct 23 2023

WARMUP	3 x 300
	#1 White/Pink @ 3:50/3:55
	#2 (50 Pink/50 max of 4 breaths) @ 4:00
	#3 No Breath in or out of walls
	3 x { w/fins
	    25 underwater kick @ :30
	    50 Back descend @ :50
	    75 Fast Kick - Flutter @ 1:00/1:10
	    100 FAST @ 2:00
	    }

SPRINT	1 x 300 white
	2 x {
	    100 Red from Blocks
	    200 white
	    100 MAX from push
	    100 white
	    }
	2 x {
	    50 Red from Blocks
	    100 white
	    50 MAX from Push
	    50 white
	    }

DISTANCE	4 x 100 IM pink @ 1:50 1 x 200 Broken each 50 for :10 (1:00) 3 x 50 MAX from a dive @ 2:30 rest 4 x 25 MAX breakout @ :10 rest 1 x 400 White @ 4:00/4:10 4 x 100 Kick D 1-4 @ 1:50 5 x 100 (25 kick BR/25 swim choice) @ 1:40
MID-DISTANCE	2 x (10 x 100 @ 2:30) ALL OUT MAX

WEEK 9	Tue Oct 24 2023
WARMUP	1 x 500 (250 Free/250 Back) 1 x 100 Scull on back, arms at side 1 x 100 Scull on front, arms at side 1 x 300 Scull 4 x 50 Dolphin on Back @ :50 4 x 100 (Kick/Drill) Worst Stroke @ 1:50 1 x 700 Paddle/Pull
MAIN SET	4 x 100 IM @ 1:25 4 x 50 Fast Kick @ 1:00 1 x 200 white 10 x 100 MAX Kick @ 1:40 500 Cooldown

WEEK 9	Wed Oct 25 2023

WARMUP	400 IM
	8 x 50 Kick @ :10 rest
	10 x 100 @ :15 rest
	Odds: Fly
	Evens: Free
	3 x {
	   1 x 300 – Catchup Drill
	   5 x 50 drill – Choice @ 1:10
	   4 x 25 Stroke @:40
	}
	10 x 50 w/fins 25 underwater kick/25 swim @ 1:00
	4 x 25 underwater kick @ :40

SPRINT	1 x 200 (100 Red/100 Pink) (:30) 4 x 100 JMI @ 1:00/1:10 1 x 300 (100 White/100 Pink/100 Red) (:30) 4 x 75 JMI @ :50/:55 2 x 200 (100 Pink/100 Red) @ 2:30 (1:00) 3 x 100 Best Average @ 2:00
DISTANCE	5 x 500's (white - pink - red - blue - Max for time)
MID-DISTANCE	8 x 50 w/fins (12.5 underwater Kick Red/12.5 Swim no breath/25 easy) @ 1:00 (1:00) 8 x 25 @ :40 odds: Build evens: Accelerate 8 x 100 Negative Split (50 White/50 Blue) @ 1:20FR/1:30 FR (1:00) 5 x 100 MAX Kick @ 2:00 (3:00) 8 x 100 @ 1:25/1:30 (2) Pink-(2) Red-(2) Blue- (2) MAX (1:00) 5 x 100 Pull Blue @ 1:30 (3:00)

WEEK 9	Thu Oct 26 2023
WARMUP	1 x 500 Free RB5 3 x 100 Kick 3 x 100 Free RB5 4 x 50 Descend Kick @ 1:00 (1:00) 8 x 50 Kick w/fins @ :40 1 x 300 Free Easy 4 x 200 @ 2:30/2:40 First 50 build to MAX turn + 3 Strokes breakout no breath (1:00) 4 x 100 @ 1:25/1:30 (25 no breath Red/75 Choice)
MAIN SET	2 x 300 @ 3:40/3:50 #1 Negative Split – White/Pink #2 Negative Split – White/Red 8 x 100 JMI #1-4 @ 1:20/1:25 #5-8 @ 1:10/1:15

WEEK 9	Fri Oct 27 2023
WARMUP	400 Kick 8 x 100 Choice @ :15 rest 8 x 25 w/fins FAST underwater kick @ :40 1 x 400 Kick White @ 7:00 4 x 50 (25 Blue/ 25 white) @ :50
SPRINT	15 x 100 #1-3 Free @ 1:30 #4-6 Build each 50 to MAX flip @ 1:30 #7-9 Kick @ 2:00 #10-12 (50 BK/50 Scull) @ 1:50 #13-15 D1-3 to Pink @ 1:30 400 Kick 4 x 50 Kick Descend
DISTANCE	6 x 25 (Drill/Build/Drill/Build/Drill/Sprint) @ :40 2x Broken 200's (:20 secs each 100) 2 x Broken 100 (@ each 50 for :10 seconds) 1 x Broken 100 (@ each 25 for :10 seconds) 4 x 50 MAX @ :40 #1-2 max of 3 breaths #3-4 max of 2 breaths

MID-DISTANCE	1 x 600 Paddle w/Pull Buoy
	10 x 100 JMI @ 1:10/1:25
	3 x {
	   1 x 75 Build @ 1:20
	   2 x 50 @ :50
	   1 x 500 Paddle w/Pull Buoy
	   2 x 200 @ 2:30/2:40
	   Pink-Red
	}
	2 x {
	   600 Choice
	   6 x 50 @ 1:00
	   White/Pink/Red/Blue/Max/Max
	}

WEEK 9	Sat Oct 28 2023
WARMUP	400 RIMO 6 x 100 Non-Free (50 Kick/50 Swim) @ :10 rest 3 x 300 Paddle w/Pull Buoy @ 4:15 (:30) 3 x 100 Non-Free work walls @ 1:40 6 x 50 Fist Drill @ 1:00 6 x 25 Build @ :30
MAIN SET	4 x 50 Kick Descend to MAX @ :55 (1:00) 2 x 500 @ 5:30/6:00 Pink - Red 4 x 50 Kick D1-4 at MAX @ 1:00 (2:00) 2 x 300 @ 3:30/3:45 Red-MAX 4 x 50 Kick Dolphin on back @ 1:00 2 x 800 @ 10:00/11:00 White-Pink-Red-White by 100s

OCTOBER-NOVEMBER   ELITE SWIM WORKOUT '24   WEEK 10

Monday	Tuesday	Wednesday	Thursday	Friday	Saturday
1 x 200 Free 3 x 100 Free RB5 1 x 200 Free 3 x 100 Free RB6	300 Choice 200 Free 4 x 100 Kick @ :20 rest	4 x 200 Free-NonFree-Back/BR by 50's-Kick	1 x 800 (200 Free/300 Kick/200 NonFree/100 Drill) 2 x 400 #1 IM #2 Kick choice	500 Choice 200 IM 8 x 50 Kick @ :10 rest	4 x 200 Paddle w/Pull Buoy @ 2:20/2:30/2:40 1 x 400 Kick White @ 7:00 1 x 200 Drill
6 x 50 Fist Drill @ 1:00 6 x 25 Build to great finish @ :30	10 x 100 #1-3 Free @ 1:30 #4-6 100 IM @ 1:40 #7-10 (25 No breath/50 Swim/25 1RB:1) @ 1:40	10 x 50 Kick @ :55 1 x 400 IM w/Fins 4 x 25 sprint kick @ :50	1 x 200 Kick MAX for time @ 4:00 4 x 50 kick easy @ 1:10 1 x 100 Kick MAX for time (dolphin on back)	2 x (100 Drill #1 Stroke @ 1:50 2 x 75 (White/Pink/Blue) @ 1:10 2 x 50 @ :35/:450 2 x 25 underwater kick @ :30 }	1 x 200 w/fins 4 x 50 @ 1650 Pace @ 1:00 1 x Broken 500 @ :10 rest 4 x (
2 x (1 x 300 Kick (150 White w/board/150 Pink no board) @ 5:45 4 x 50 Descend to MAX @ 1:00 4 x 25 Dolphin on back @ :30 }	4 x 200 Free-Non Free-Kick no board-RIMO	SPRINT 8 x 75 Paddle w/Pull Buoy @ 1:15 4 x 25 (drill,build,drill,sprint) @ :40 2 x Broken 100 @ 25's 200 white	8 x 100 JMI @ 1:15/1:20 4 x 25 Blue no breath @ :30 4 x 200 @ 2:20/2:30 odds: Ascend starting at Red evens: Descend to Max (2:00) 3 x 100 @ 1:00/1:05	4 x 150 Kick (White/Pink/Build to MAX finish) @ 2:15	4 x 100 Neg Split @ 1:30 (White/Pink) 4 x 50 Descend 4 x 25 Build }
SPRINT	4 x 50 Free @ :35/:40 4 x 100 Free @ 1:10/1:20 4 x 50 Free @ :35/:40 4 x 100 JMI @ 1:00/1:05/1:10/1:15 200 white	6 x 100 (swim/kick/non-free/Choice) @ 1:40 10 x 50 @ 1:40	1 x 300 JMI @ 4:00/4:20 2 x 200 Kick @ 4:00/4:20 #1 Flutter #2 Dolphin 4 x 50 Red Swim @ 1:10/1:15	SPRINT	
4 x 100 (50 Drill/ 50 build to max finish) @ 1:30		DISTANCE 8 x 100 Paddle w/Pull Buoy @ 1:15 4 x 25 (drill,build,drill,sprint) @ :40		3 x 200 Paddle/Pull @ 2:45 3 x 100 Pull @ 1:20 6 x 25 w/ fins (12.5 underwater MAX kick) @ :30	
1 x Broken 200 @ 50 2 x 100 MAX Cool Down		1 x Broken 100 @ 25's or 200 @ 50's 2 x 50 10 x 75 @ 1:15 # 1-4 (swim/kick/non-free) # 5-8 (easy,medium,build to fast finish) # 9-10 Pink		4 x 50 Max @ 3:00 4 x 25 blue	
DISTANCE 4 x 200 (White/Pink/Red/Blue) @ 2:20/2:30/2:40/2:50/3:00 8 x 100 @ 1:20/1:25/1:40 D1-4 , 5-8 Hold Time (2:00) 3 x 200 (Red/Blue/MAX) @ 2:30/2:40/2:50 6 x 100 Best Average @ 1:25/1:40 MID-DISTANCE		4 x 100 (50 Kick/50 swim) @ 1:40		1 x 400 white 2 x (5 x 50 Best Average) @ 1:30 second round w/ fins DISTANCE	
1 x 600 Free 1 x 400 IM 8 x 50 IMO x 2 @ :10 rest		MID-DISTANCE 8 x 100 Paddle/Pull @ 1:20/1:30		12 x 50 JMI @ :35/:40 Build each 50 to Pink – no breath from flags to wall on finish MID-DISTANCE	
6 x 150 (Drill/Kick/Swim) @ 2:15 5 x 50 fist #1 Stroke @ 1:00 4 x 25 build to pink @ :30		3 x (300 + 100 easy) White-Pink-Red (2:00		5 x (200 Best Average @ /3:20 4 x 50 Avg. Best time 200 Pace @ 1:00 (1:00 rest) }	
1 x 400 IM @ 5:10/5:30/6:00/6:30 4 x 50 Kick no board IMO @ :45/:50 4 x 200 IM @ 3:00/3:15/3:30/3:40 8 x 50 kick no board #1 Stroke @ :50		8 x (75 + 25 easy) White-Pink-Red-White x 2			
8 x 50 Chutes @ 1:15/1:20 10 x 50 w/ fins (12.5 underwater kick/12.5 swim) @ 1:00		10 x (50 + 50 easy) Hold 500 Goal pace			

WEEK 10	Mon Oct 30 2023

WARMUP	1 x 200 Free
	3 x 100 Free RB5
	1 x 200 Free
	3 x 100 Free RB6
	6 x 50 Fist Drill @ 1:00
	6 x 25 Build to great finish @ :30
	2 x {
	   1 x 300 Kick (150 White w/board/150 Pink no board) @ 5:45
	   4 x 50 Descend to MAX @ 1:00
	   4 x 25 Dolphin on back @ :30

SPRINT	4 x 100 (50 Drill/ 50 build to max finish) @ 1:30 1 x Broken 200 @ 50 2 x 100 MAX Cool Down
DISTANCE	4 x 200 (White/Pink/Red/Blue) @ 2:20/2:30/2:40/2:50/3:00 8 x 100 @ 1:20/1:25/1:40 D1-4 , 5-8 Hold Time (2:00) 3 x 200 (Red/Blue/MAX) @ 2:30/2:40/2:50 6 x 100 Best Average @ 1:25/1:40
MID-DISTANCE	1 x 600 Free 1 x 400 IM 8 x 50 IMO x 2 @ :10 rest 6 x 150 (Drill/Kick/Swim) @ 2:15 5 x 50 fist #1 Stroke @ 1:00 4 x 25 build to pink @ :30 1 x 400 IM @ 5:10/5:30/6:00/6:30 4 x 50 Kick no board IMO @ :45/:50 4 x 200 IM @ 3:00/3:15/3:30/3:40 8 x 50 kick no board #1 Stroke @ :50 8 x 50 Chutes @ 1:15/1:20 10 x 50 w/ fins (12.5 underwater kick/12.5 swim) @ 1:00

WEEK 10	Tue Oct 31 2023
WARMUP	300 Choice 200 Free 4 x 100 Kick @ :20 rest 10 x 100 #1-3 Free @ 1:30 #4-6 100 IM @ 1:40 #7-10 (25 No breath/50 Swim/25 1RB:1) @ 1:40 4 x 200 Free-Non Free-Kick no board-RIMO
MAIN SET	4 x 50 Free @ :35/:40 4 x 100 Free @ 1:10/1:20 4 x 50 Free @ :35/:40 4 x 100 JMI @ 1:00/1:05/1:10/1:15 200 white

WEEK 10	Wed Nov 01 2023
WARMUP	4 x 200 Free-NonFree-Back/BR by 50's-Kick 10 x 50 Kick @ :55 1 x 400 IM w/Fins 4 x 25 sprint kick @ :50
SPRINT	8 x 75 Paddle w/Pull Buoy @ 1:15 4 x 25 (drill,build,drill,sprint) @ :40 2 x Broken 100 @ 25's 200 white 6 x 100 (swim/kick/non-free/Choice) @ 1:40 10 x 50 @ 1:40
DISTANCE	8 x 100 Paddle w/Pull Buoy @ 1:15 4 x 25 (drill,build,drill,sprint) @ :40 1 x Broken 100 @ 25's or 200 @ 50's 2 x 50 10 x 75 @ 1:15 # 1-4 (swim/kick/non-free) # 5-8 (easy,medium,build to fast finish) # 9-10 Pink 4 x 100 (50 Kick/50 swim) @ 1:40
MID-DISTANCE	8 x 100 Paddle/Pull @ 1:20/1:30 3 x (300 + 100 easy) White-Pink-Red (2:00 8 x (75 + 25 easy) White-Pink-Red-White x 2 10 x (50 + 50 easy) Hold 500 Goal pace

WEEK 10	Thu Nov 02 2023
WARMUP	1 x 800 (200 Free/300 Kick/200 NonFree/100 Drill) 2 x 400 #1 IM #2 Kick choice
MAIN SET	8 x 100 JMI @ 1:15/1:20 4 x 25 Blue no breath @ :30 4 x 200 @ 2:20/2:30 odds: Ascend starting at Red evens: Descend to Max (2:00) 3 x 100 @ 1:00/1:05 1 x 300 JMI @ 4:00/4:20 2 x 200 Kick @ 4:00/4:20 #1 Flutter #2 Dolphin 4 x 50 Red Swim @ 1:10/1:15 1 x 200 Kick MAX for time @ 4:00 4 x 50 kick easy @ 1:10 1 x 100 Kick MAX for time (dolphin on back)

WEEK 10	Fri Nov 03 2023

WARMUP	500 Choice
	200 IM
	8 x 50 Kick @ :10 rest
	
	2 x {
	   100 Drill #1 Stroke @ 1:50
	   2 x 75 (White/Pink/Blue) @ 1:10
	   2 x 50 @ :35/:450
	   2 x 25 underwater kick @ :30
	}
	4 x 150 Kick (White/Pink/Build to MAX finish) @ 2:15

SPRINT	3 x 200 Paddle/Pull @ 2:45 3 x 100 Pull @ 1:20 6 x 25 w/ fins (12.5 underwater MAX kick) @ :30 4 x 50 Max @ 3:00 4 x 25 blue 1 x 400 white 2 x (5 x 50 Best Average) @ 1:30 second round w/ fins
DISTANCE	8 x 100 Paddle w/Pull Buoy @ 1:15 4 x 25 (drill,build,drill,sprint) @ :40 1 x Broken 100 @ 25's or 200 @ 50's 2 x 50 10 x 75 @ 1:15 # 1-4 (swim/kick/non-free) # 5-8 (easy,medium,build to fast finish) # 9-10 Pink 4 x 100 (50 Kick/50 swim) @ 1:40 12 x 50 JMI @ :35/:40 Build each 50 to Pink – no breath from flags to wall on finish

MID-DISTANCE	5 x {
	   200 Best Average @ /3:20
	   4 x 50 Avg. Best time 200 Pace @ 1:00
	   (1:00 rest)
	}

WEEK 10	Sat Nov 04 2023
WARMUP	4 x 200 Paddle w/Pull Buoy @ 2:20/2:30/2:40 1 x 400 Kick White @ 7:00 1 x 200 Drill 1 x 200 w/fins

MAIN SET	4 x 50 @ 1650 Pace @ 1:00
	1 x Broken 500 @ :10 rest
	4 x {
	   4 x 100 Neg Split @ 1:30
	   (White/Pink)
	   4 x 50 Descend
	   4 x 25 Build
	}

NOVEMBER — ELITE SWIM WORKOUT '24 — WEEK 11

Monday	Tuesday	Wednesday	Thursday	Friday	Saturday

200 SKIMPS
12 x 50 Drill IMO x 3 @1:00
 	
5 x 200 :20
#1 Kick
#2 Paddle w/Pull Buoy White
#3 Paddle w/Pull Buoy Pink
#4 Paddle w/Pull Buoy Red
#5 Kick
 	
SPRINT
4 x 300 w/fins @ 3:45
2 x {
4 x 100 @ 125
#1-2 Descend each 100 to Pink
#3-4 Descend each 100
}
4 x 50's MAX @ 3:00
4 x 25's MAX @ 2:00
 	
4 x 125 Neg Split (75 White/75 Red) @ 2:00
4 x 100 Descend to MAX @ 1:30
4 x 100 Best Average @ 1:30
 	
DISTANCE
2 x {
1 x 500 Red
(2:00)
1 x 300 Red
(2:00)
1 x 100 Red
(2:00)
}
1 x 300 cool down
 	
MID-DISTANCE
2 x {
1 x 500 Pink + 100 easy
1 x 400 Red + 100 easy
1 x 300 Blue + 100 easy
1 x 200 Red + 100 easy
1 x 100 MAX + 100 easy
}
	1 x 500 Free
	1 x 300 Scull
	
	2 x 100 Paddle w/Pull Buoy @ 2:30/2:40
	4 x 100 Pull @ 1:30
	4 x 75 Stroke (long underwater on each wall) @ 1:20
	4 x 50 25 build to top speed, 25 easy @ 1:00
	
	2 x {
	1 x 200 kick White
	5 x 50 Kick D 1-5
	}
	6 x 150 @ 2:00/2:10
	#1-3 Negative Split
	#4-6 Best average
	(2:00)
	5 x 100 JMI @ 1:00/1:05/1:10
		400 Back
		200 Free
		200 Kick
		
		2 x 200 Scull #1 Front, #2 Back
		4 x 50 Fist Drill @ 1:00
		4 x 75 (fist drill/swim/build) @ 1:10
		
		SPRINT
		6 x 50 @ 4:00
		#1-2 MAX 2 Breaths TOTAL
		#3-4 MAX 1 Breath TOTAL
		#5-6 MAX 0 Breath TOTAL
		
		4 x 25 MAX w/ fins from dive
		1 x 50 w/ fins from push
		
		DISTANCE
		8 x 50 build to great finish @ 1:00
		
		1 x 300 MAX
		3 x 100 MAX @ 5:00
		
		10 x 50 @ 1:00
		Odds 50 Kick
		Evens 50 Swim
		
		MID-DISTANCE
		3 x 500 Best Time + 30 @ 5:30/6:00/6:20
		(2:00)
		8 x 200 Best Average @ 2:20/2:30
		(2:00)
			2 x 200 #1 Free, #2 Non-Free
			4 x 100 IM :20 sec6 x 50 @ 1:00 2 fist drill, 1 build3 x 100 Kick @ 1:50
			Sprint
			
			10 x 50 Back Drill @ :55
			2 x 200 Paddles
			4 x 50 kick @ :50
			
			3 x 200 IM @ 3:00/3:10
			3 x 200 (Kick no Board/Kick board /Choice) (1:00)
			4 x 25 underwater kick @ :45
			4 x 25 underwater with arms @ :40
			4 x 25 (1/2 way underwater MAX kick + breakout/white) @ :30
			3 x 200 IM :30 sec
			6 x 100 JMI @ 1:05/1:10/1:15 (1:00)
			2 x 100 JMI @ 1:00/1:05/1:10
				2 x 200
				#1 Kick Choice
				#2 Kick no Board
				6 x 75 @ 1:20
				50 drill/25 swim
				
				10 x 25 w/ chutes @ :45 Red
				10 x 25 x/ fins MAX underwater kick @ :30
				2 x {
				4 x 200 @ 2:30
				}
				
				SPRINT
				6 x 100 (white/pink/red/blue) @ 1:25
				
				8 x 25 from a dive w/ 5 Strokes fast @ 1:00 rest
				
				1 x 100 Broken @ the 50 and the 75 @ 4:00 rest
				2 x 50 MAX from a dive @ 2:30 rest
				4 x 25's Max start + breakout, white remainder
				
				DISTANCE
				1 x 500 White @ 6:30/7:00
				4 x 100 Kick D 1-4 @ 1:50
				5 x 50 (25 kick BR/25 swim choice) @ 1:00
				
				DISTANCE
				4 x 100 IM @ 1:50 Pink
				
				12 x 50 Fins @ :40
				4 x 50 #1 drill, #2 build, #3 drill, #4 sprint @ :30
				
				- 2 Minutes between rounds
				3 x {
				200 White @ 2:40
				2 x 75 Pink @ 1:30
				4 x 50 Red @ 1:00
				2 x 25 MAX @ :40
				}
				
				MID-DISTANCE
				10 x 50 @ 4:00
				#1-3 MAX of 3 Breaths
				#4-6 MAX of 2 Breaths
				#7-10 MAX of 1 Breath
				
				4 x (75 - 25 easy)
				Descend
				8 x (50 + 50 easy)
				Round 1 all red
				Round 2 all MAX
					4 x 200 @ :15 rest
					odds: Free
					evens: (50 breast drill/50 Choice)
					
					3 x 300 paddle only BP 3-5-7 by 100's @ 3:50
					
					4 x 200 Fin Kick @ 2:45
					4 x 100 Fin Kick @ 1:20
					3 x {
					300 Non-Free @ :20 rest
					200 Swim – Pink @ 2:30
					100 Swim – Red @ 2:00
					}
					4 x 200 (free/fly by 100s) @ 2:50
					8 x 100 @ 1:25
					odds: Free
					evens: Fly
					(2:00)
					3 x 200 (free/fly) @ 2:40
					6 x 100 fly @ 1:40

WEEK 11	Mon Nov 06 2023
WARMUP	200 SKIMPS 12 x 50 Drill IMO x 3 @ 1:00 5 x 200 :20 #1 Kick #2 Paddle w/Pull Buoy White #3 Paddle w/Pull Buoy Pink #4 Paddle w/Pull Buoy Red #5 Kick

SPRINT	4 x 300 w/fins @ 3:45
	2 x {
	    4 x 100 @ 1:25
	    #1-2 Descend each 100 to Pink
	    #3-4 Descend each 100
	}
	4 x 50's MAX @ 3:00
	4 x 25's MAX @ 2:00
	
	4 x 125 Neg Split (75 White/75 Red) @ 2:00
	4 x 100 Descend to MAX @ 1:30
	4 x 100 Best Average @ 1:30

DISTANCE	2 x {
	    1 x 500 Red
	    (2:00)
	    1 x 300 Red
	    (2:00)
	    1 x 100 Red
	    (2:00)
	     }
	
	1 x 300 cool down

MID-DISTANCE	2 x {
	    1 x 500 Pink + 100 easy
	    1 x 400 Red + 100 easy
	    1 x 300 Blue + 100 easy
	    1 x 200 Red + 100 easy
	    1 x 100 MAX + 100 easy
	}

WEEK 10	Tue Nov 07 2023
WARMUP	1 x 500 Free 1 x 300 Scull 2 x 100 Paddle w/Pull Buoy @ 2:30/2:40 4 x 100 Pull @ 1:30 4 x 75 Stroke (long underwater on each wall) @ 1:20 4 x 50 25 build to top speed, 25 easy @ 1:00

MAIN SET	2 x {
	1 x 200 kick White
	5 x 50 Kick D 1-5
	}
	
	6 x 150 @ 2:00/2:10
	#1-3 Negative Split
	#4-6 Best average
	(2:00)
	5 x 100 JMI @ 1:00/1:05/1:10

WEEK 11	Wed Nov 08 2023
WARMUP	400 Back 200 Free 200 Kick 2 x 200 Scull #1 Front, #2 Back 4 x 50 Fist Drill @ 1:00 4 x 75 (fist drill/swim/build) @ 1:10
SPRINT	6 x 50 @ 4:00 #1-2 MAX 2 Breaths TOTAL #3-4 MAX 1 Breath TOTAL #5-6 MAX 0 Breath TOTAL 4 x 25 MAX w/ fins from dive 1 x 50 w/ fins from push
DISTANCE	8 x 50 build to great finish @ 1:00 1 x 300 MAX 3 x 100 MAX @ 5:00 10 x 50 @ 1:00 Odds 50 Kick Evens 50 Swim
MID-DISTANCE	3 x 500 Best Time + 30 @ 5:30/6:00/6:20 (2:00) 8 x 200 Best Average @ 2:20/2:30 (2:00)

WEEK 10	Thu Nov 09 2023
WARMUP	2 x 200 #1 Free, #2 Non-Free 4 x 100 IM :20 sec6 x 50 @ 1:00 2 fist drill, 1 build3 x 100 Kick @ 1:50 Sprint 10 x 50 Back Drill @ :55 2 x 200 Paddles 4 x 50 kick @ :50 3 x 200 IM @ 3:00/3:10 3 x 200 (Kick no Board/Kick board /Choice)
MAIN SET	4 x 25 underwater kick @ :45 4 x 25 underwater with arms @ :40 4 x 25 (1/2 way underwater MAX kick + breakout/white) @ :30 (1:00) 3 x 200 IM :30 sec 6 x 100 JMI @ 1:05/1:10/1:15 (1:00) 2 x 100 JMI @ 1:00/1:05/1:10

WEEK 11	Fri Nov 10 2023

WARMUP	2 x 200
	#1 Kick Choice
	#2 Kick no Board
	200 IM
	6 x 75 @ 1:20
	50 drill/25 swim
	10 x 25 w/ chutes @ :45 Red
	10 x 25 x/ fins MAX underwater kick @ :30
	2 x {
	   4 x 200 @ 2:30
	   (1:00)
	}

SPRINT	6 x 100 (white/pink/red/blue) @ 1:25 8 x 25 from a dive w/ 5 Strokes fast @ 1:00 rest 1 x 100 Broken @ the 50 and the 75 @ 4:00 rest 2 x 50 MAX from a dive @ 2:30 rest 4 x 25's Max start + breakout, white remainder 1 x 500 White @ 6:30/7:00 4 x 100 Kick D 1-4 @ 1:50 5 x 50 (25 kick BR/25 swim choice) @ 1:00

DISTANCE	4 x 100 IM @ 1:50 Pink
	
	12 x 50 Fins @ :40
	4 x 50 #1 drill, #2 build, #3 drill, #4 sprint @ :30
	– 2 Minutes between rounds
	3 x {
	   200 White @ 2:40
	   2 x 75 Pink @ 1:30
	   4 x 50 Red @ 1:00
	   2 x 25 MAX @ :40
	}

MID-DISTANCE	10 x 50 @ 4:00 #1-3 MAX of 3 Breaths #4-6 MAX of 2 Breaths #7-10 MAX of 1 Breath 4 x (75+ 25 easy) Descend 8 x (50 + 50 easy) Round 1 all red Round 2 all MAX

WEEK 10	Sat Nov 11 2023
WARMUP	4 x 200 @ :15 rest odds: Free evens: (50 breast drill/50 Choice) 3 x 300 paddle only BP 3-5-7 by 100's @ 3:50 4 x 200 Fin Kick @ 2:45 4 x 100 Fin Kick @ 1:20

MAIN SET	3 x {
	   300 Non-Free @ :20 rest
	   200 Swim – Pink @ 2:30
	   100 Swim – Red @ 2:00
	}
	
	4 x 200 (free/fly by 100s) @ 2:50
	8 x 100 @ 1:25
	odds: Free
	evens: Fly
	(2:00)
	3 x 200 (free/fly) @ 2:40
	6 x 100 fly @ 1:40

NOVEMBER   ELITE SWIM WORKOUT '24   WEEK 12

Monday	Tuesday	Wednesday	Thursday	Friday	Saturday
1 x 600 (300 Free-300 NonFree)	500 Free	200 SKIMPS	3 x 600	200 SKIMPS	8 x 125
4 x 100 IMO (drill fly) @ :10 rest	3 x 100 Kick w/Board	1 x 500 Kick	#1 200 RIMO/200 Swim/200 Drill		odds: 25 Free/50 Kick no board/50 Non-Free
8 x 50 (Fly/Free, Back/Free, Breast/Free, Free/Free) @	10 x 100 IM Order @ :15 rest		#2 300 (50 drill/50 swim best Stroke/300 kick)	1 x 400 Paddle w/Pull Buoy @ 5:10	evens: 50 Free/75 Kick
		8 x 50 (25 Drill/ 25 build to max finish) @ :50	#3 Swim Choice	8 x 50 Pull (2 best: Stroke, 1 Free) @ :50/1:00	
1000 Kick w/Board	5 x 100 (Kick/Drill/Swim/Drill) @ 2:00	5 x 100 Stroke @ 1:10/1:20/1:30/1:40			1 x 200 Scull on Back
2 x 200 IMO	1 x 400 IMO w/Fins		8 x 100 @ 1:40	6 x 100	1 x 200 Scull on Front
	4 x 25 underwater kick @ :30	SPRINT	#1-3 (50 Kick Red/50 Kick White)	#1-3 (Kick/Drill/Swim) @ 2:00	
SPRINT		5 x 100 Kick w/fins @ 1:15	#4-7 (75 Kick Pink/25 Kick MAX)	#4-6 Past flags on each wall @ 2:00	20 x 25
12 x 25 @ :55	SPRINT	4 x 200 Paddle w/Pull Buoy	#8 100 Kick MAX		#1-10 w/ chutes @ :45
5 x 50 MAX @ 4:00	2 x 500 @ 5:40/6:00	6 x 50		SPRINT	#11-20 MAX w/ fins underwater kick @ :40
#1-4 max of 1 breath	#1 (250 White/ 250 Pink)	odds: Red @ 1:00	2 x 300 Free JMI @ 3:15/3:30	8 x 50	
#10 No Breath	#2 (250 Red/ 250 Clear) (1:00)	evens: white @ 1:00	4 x 50 Kick MAX @ 1:00	2 red @ 1:00	1 x 200 Work breakout on each wall @ 3:00
	4 x 100 @ 1:30	200 clear	2 x 300 Free JMI @ 2:05/2:15 (1:00)	1 white @ 1:20	4 x 50 Dolphin on Back @ 1:00
300 white	White-Pink-Red-Blue	10 x 50 @ 1:30 MAX PACE	4 x 50 Kick MAX @ 1:00		4 x 25 Build @ :30
	2 x 500 @ 5:40/6:00			3 x {	
DISTANCE	#1 (250 White/250 Red)	DISTANCE		1 x 25 MAX from Dive @ :30	3 x {
5 x 100 @ 1:30	#2 (250 Blue/250 White)	2 x (300 + 100 easy)		1 x 75 JMI @ 1:10/1:15	1 x 25 MAX :30 rest
	4 x 100 @ 1:30	Pink – Pink		1 x 50 kick ½ way underwater on every wall @ :40/:45	1 x 50 MAX Kick :45-1:00 rest
1 x 400 DPS @ 5:20	Pink-Red-Blue-MAX	4 x (200 + 50 easy)		1 x 25 MAX underwater kick from Dive @ :40	1 x 50 MAX Dive
8 x 50 (2 white/ 2 red/ 2 pink) @ :50 (:30)		Descend		1 x 100 MAX for time	}
1 x 400 pull @ 5:00		4 x (100 + 50 easy)		}	1 x 500 Free
3 x 100 (2) White (1) Pink (:30)		D 1-4			5 x 50 Non-Free @ :50
1 x 400 pull @ 5:00		8 x (50 + 50 easy)		DISTANCE	
5 x 100 blue @ 1:20		Hold Goal 500 Pace		6 x 100 (white/pink/red/blue) @ 1:25	
				8 x 25 from a dive w/ 5 Strokes fast @ 1:00 rest	
MID-DISTANCE		MID-DISTANCE			
6 x 100 @ 1:30		1 x 300 w/fins		1 x 100 Broken @ the 50 and the 75 @ 4:00 rest	
1 x 400 DPS @ 5:00		4 x 50 @ 1650 Pace @ 1:00		2 x 50 MAX from a dive @ 3:00 rest	
8 x 50 (2 white/ 2 red/ 2 pink) @ :50 (:30)		1 x Broken 200 @ 50s for :10 rest		4 x 25's Max start + breakout, easy finish	
1 x 400 DPS @ 5:00		2 x {			
5 x 100 blue @ 1:20 (:30)		4 x 100 Neg Split @ 1:30 (White/Pink)		1 x 500 White @ 6:30/7:00	
1 x 300 Negative Split @ 4:00		4 x 50 Descend		4 x 100 Kick D 1-4 @ 1:50	
8 x 25 Build to MAX finish @ :30		4 x 25 Build		5 x 50 (25 kick BR/25 swim choice) @ 1:00	
		4 x 150 (breast/free/choice)			
Cooldown		}		MID-DISTANCE	
				1 x 400 Build each 100 to MAX flip3 200 Red @ 2:30/2:40	
				4 x 150 (100 Build to Pink + 50 Red)	
				3 x 100 (50 Kick/50 Swim) @ 1:40	

WEEK 12	Mon Nov 13 2023
WARMUP	1 x 600 (300 Free-300 NonFree) 4 x 100 IMO (drill fly) @ :10 rest 8 x 50 (Fly/Free, Back/Free, Breast/Free, Free/Free) @ 1000 Kick w/Board 2 x 200 IMO
SPRINT	12 x 25 @ :55 5 x 50 MAX @ 4:00 #1-4 max of 1 breath #10 No Breath 300 white
DISTANCE	5 x 100 @ 1:30 1 x 400 DPS @ 5:20 8 x 50 (2 white/ 2 pink/ 2 red/ 2 pink) @ :50 (:30) 1 x 400 pull @ 5:00 3 x 100 (2) White (1) Pink (:30) 1 x 400 pull @ 5:00 5 x 100 blue @ 1:20
MID-DISTANCE	6 x 100 @ 1:30 1 x 400 DPS @ 5:00 8 x 50 (2 white/ 2 pink/ 2 red/ 2 pink) @ :50 (:30) 1 x 400 DPS @ 5:00 5 x 100 blue @ 1:20 (:30) 1 x 300 Negative Split @ 4:00 8 x 25 Build to MAX finish @ :30

WEEK 12	Tue Nov 14 2023
WARMUP	500 Free 3 x 100 Kick w/Board 10 x 100 IM Order @ :15 rest 5 x 100 (Kick/Drill/Swim/Drill) @ 2:00 1 x 400 IMO w/Fins 4 x 25 underwater kick @ :30
MAIN SET	2 x 500 @ 5:40/6:00 #1 (250 White/ 250 Pink) #2 (250 Red/ 250 Clear) (1:00) 4 x 100 @ 1:30 White-Pink-Red-Blue 2 x 500 @ 5:40/6:00 #1 (250 White/250 Red) #2 (250 Blue/250 White) 4 x 100 @ 1:30 Pink-Red-Blue-MAX

WEEK 12	Wed Nov 15 2023
WARMUP	200 SKIMPS 1 x 500 Kick 8 x 50 (25 Drill / 25 build to max finish) @ :50 5 x 100 Stroke @ 1:10/1:20/1:30/1:40
SPRINT	5 x 100 Kick w/fins @ 1:15 4 x 200 Paddle w/Pull Buoy 6 x 50 odds: Red @ 1:00 evens: white @ 1:00 200 clear 10 x 50 @ 1:30 MAX PACE
DISTANCE	2 x (300 + 100 easy) Pink – Pink 4 x (200 + 50 easy) Descend 4 x (100 + 50 easy) D 1-4 8 x (50 + 50 easy) Hold Goal 500 Pace

MID-DISTANCE	1 x 300 w/fins
	4 x 50 @ 1650 Pace @ 1:00
	
	1 x Broken 200 @ 50s for :10 rest
	2 x {
	   4 x 100 Neg Split @ 1:30
	   (White/Pink)
	   4 x 50 Descend
	   4 x 25 Build
	   4 x 150 (breast/free/choice)
	}

WEEK 12	Thu Nov 16 2023
WARMUP	3 x 600 #1 200 RIMO / 200 Swim / 200 Drill #2 300 (50 drill / 50 swim best Stroke / 300 kick) #3 Swim Choice
MAIN SET	8 x 100 @ 1:45 #1-3 (50 Kick Red / 50 Kick White) #4-7 (75 Kick Pink / 25 Kick MAX) #8 100 Kick MAX 2 x 300 Free JMI @ 3:15 / 3:30 4 x 50 Kick MAX @ 1:00 (1:00) 2 x 300 Free JMI @ 3:05 / 3:15 4 x 50 Kick MAX @ 1:00

WEEK 12	Fri Nov 17 2023
WARMUP	200 SKIMPS 1 x 400 Paddle w/Pull Buoy @ 5:10 8 x 50 Pull (2 best Stroke, 1 Free) @ :50/1:00 6 x 100 #1-3 (Kick/Drill/Swim) @ 2:00 #4-6 Past flags on each wall @ 2:00

SPRINT	8 x 50
	2 red @ 1:00
	1 white @ 1:20
	3 x {
	   1 x 25 MAX from Dive @ :30
	   1 x 75 JMI @ 1:10/1:15
	   1 x 50 kick ½ way underwater on every wall @ :40/:45
	   1 x 25 MAX underwater kick from Dive @ :40
	   1 x 100 MAX for time
	}

DISTANCE	6 x 100 (white/pink/red/blue) @ 1:25 8 x 25 from a dive w/ 5 Strokes fast @ 1:00 rest 1 x 100 Broken @ the 50 and the 75 @ 4:00 rest 2 x 50 MAX from a dive @ 3:00 rest 4 x 25's Max start + breakout, easy finish 1 x 500 White @ 6:30/7:00 4 x 100 Kick D 1-4 @ 1:50 5 x 50 (25 kick BR/25 swim choice) @ 1:00
MID-DISTANCE	1 x 400 Build each 100 to MAX flip3 x 200 Red @ 2:30/2:40 4 x 150 (100 Build to Pink + 50 Red) 3 x 100 (50 Kick/50 Swim) @ 1:40

WEEK 12	Sat Nov 18 2023
WARMUP	8 x 125 odds: 25 Free / 50 Kick no board / 50 Non-Free evens: 50 Free / 75 Kick 1 x 200 Scull on Back 1 x 200 Scull on Front 20 x 25 #1-10 w/ chutes @ :45 #11-20 MAX w/ fins underwater kick @ :40 1 x 200 Work breakout on each wall @ 3:00 4 x 50 Dolphin on Back @ 1:00 4 x 25 Build @ :30

MAIN SET	
	
	3 x {
	   1 x 25 MAX :30 rest
	   1 x 50 MAX Kick :45-1:00 rest
	   1 x 50 MAX Dive
	}
	1 x 500 Free
	5 x 50 Non-Free @ :50

NOVEMBER ELITE SWIM WORKOUT '24 WEEK 13

Monday	Tuesday	Wednesday	Thursday	Friday	Saturday
4 x 300 Free-Kick-RIMO – (50 Swim/50 Drill)	3 x 200 #1 Free #2 (50 BK/50 Breast) #3 DPS Choice	1 x 500 (200 Free/200 Non-Free/100 RIMO) 8 x 100 @ :10 rest odds: #1 Stroke (50 drill/50 swim) evens: (50 BK/50 BR)	1 x 400 (200 Free/200 Back) 1 x 300 (150 Kick non-free/150 kick breast) 1 x 200 (100 BK/100 Choice) 1 x 100 IM	1 x 500 (200 Free/200 Non-Free/100 RIMO) 8 x 100 @ :10 rest odds: # 1 Stroke (50 drill/50 swim) evens: (50 BK/50 BR)	3 x 300 Paddle/Pull @ 3:45/4:00 BP - 5
4 x 100 IM (drill fly) @ 2:00/2:10 4 x 50 Back @ 1:00 6 x 50 (25 Breast Kick on Back) @ 1:10 4 x 75 (Free/NonFree/Free) @ 1:10 4 x 25 Breast @ :40	3 x 100 Non-Free work walls @ 1:40	8 x 100 (25 Build/50 Pink/25 Build to Fast Finish) @ 1:40 8 x 50 @ 1:00 #1-3 (1/2 underwater kick + breakout on each wall) #4-6 Build max of 3 breaths #7-8 DPS	6 x 150 Kick w/fins @ 1:45 (1:00) 8 x 50 Kick no board @ 1:00 D1-4,5-8	10 x 100 @ 1:30 odds: (25 kick/25 drill/50 swim with no breath turns) evens: DPS	3 x 300 @ 3:45/3:55 (1:00) 8 x 25 Paddles DPS – Count Stroke per 25 @ :45 4 x 25 Keep Same Stroke Count as w/ paddles per 25
	6 x 50 Fist Drill @ 1:00 6 x 25 Build @ :30		4 x 100 MAX 4 x 50 MAX 4 x 50 MAX	SPRINT	5 x 50 drill @ 1:00

SPRINT
5 x {
200 Best Average @ 3:00
4 x 50 Best Avg. @ :50 + 1:00 rest
}
	12 x 25 @ :30
	underwater kick w/fins (1:00)
	4 x 50 Dolphin on back w/fins @ :45 (:30)
	4 x 50 Dolphin on back w/fins @ :40 (:30)
		SPRINT
		6 x 75 Build @ 1:15
			12 x 50 (50 Kick/50 Swim)	2 x 300 DPS @ 4:00
				5 x 100 (3) White (2) Pink @ 1:30
				1 x 300 (150 Kick no board/ 150 Swim) @ 5:30
				5 x 100 (3) White (1) Pink (1) Red @ 1:30
					4 x 25 Kick Build each 25 @ :40
					4 x 50 Kick Descend @ :55
					4 x 25 Kick @ :30

DISTANCE 4 x (200 + 100 easy) D 1-4 4 x (75 + 25 easy) All Red 8 x (50 + 50 easy) D 1-4 , D 5-8 to MAX	1 x 400 Free @ 4:50 2 x 50 Hold Goal 200 Pace @ 1:00 1 x 400 Free @ 5:00 2 x 50 Hold Goal 200 Pace @ 1:00 1 x 400 Free @ 5:10 2 x 50 Hold Goal 200 Pace @ 1:00	1 x 400 pull @ 5:00 5 x 100 (3) White (2) Pink @ 1:30 1 x 300 (150 Kick no board/ 150 Swim) @ 5:30 5 x 50 (3) White (1) Pink (1) Red @ 1:00	4 x 100 JMI	DISTANCE 4 x 200 Pull - Kick - Pink - White 2 x 800 odd 100's: Descend even 100's Kick Pink 6 x 200 odds: Blue @ 2:20 evens: IM @ 2:40 5 x 100's (100's Descend 1-5 Red + 25 MAX)	9 x 50 (2 @ :40, 1 @ :30)

MID-DISTANCE
5 x {
400 @ 4:30/4:45/4:50
4 x 100 Goal 500 Pace @ 1:10/1:15/1:20
1:00 rest
}
		DISTANCE
		4 x 50 #1 drill, #2 build, #3 drill, #4 sprint @ :30
		
		2 x {
		1 x 100 @ 7:00
		4 x 50 @ 4:00
		}
				MID-DISTANCE
				5 x 100 Negative Split (50 White/50 Red) @ 1:20
					2 x 300 (200 Free/100 IM)
					1 x 300 Kick no board
					8 x 75 2 of each Stroke kick/drill/swim by 25s @ 1:20

		1 x 400 White 10 x 100 (50 kick/50 swim) @ 1:40 8 x 50 Non-Free @ :50		1 x Broken 500 @ 100s :10 seconds	5 x 200 Pull @ 2:30/2:45 odds: BP: 3 evens: BP: 5
		MID-DISTANCE 6 x 100 @ 1:30 1 x 400 DPS @ 5:00 8 x 50 (2 white/ 2 pink/ 2 red/ 2 pink) @ :50 (:30) 1 x 400 DPS @ 5:00 5 x 100 blue @ 1:20 (:30) 1 x 300 Negative Split @ 4:00 8 x 25 Build to MAX finish @ :30		1 x 500 (200 White/300 Pink) @ 6:30/6:45 8 x 100 (alternate free/non-free) @ 1:30 1 x 300 blue @ 4:50/5:10 6 x 100 (back/free/choice/fly) @ +:10 8 x 50 Hold 1650 Goal Pace @ :50	1 x 200 kick no board @ 3:15 4 x 75 @ 1:20 odds: white/pink/red evens:red/pink/white

					2 x {
					1 x 400 w/fins @ 5:00
					4 x 50 kick dolphin on back @ :45
					}
					16 x 25 w/fins underwater kick @ :40
					8 x 75 w/ chutes @ 1:20

WEEK 13	Mon Nov 20 2023
WARMUP	4 x 300 Free-Kick-RIMO – (50 Swim/50 Drill) 4 x 100 IM (drill fly) @ 2:00/2:10 4 x 50 Back @ 1:00 6 x 50 (25 Breast Kick on Back) @ 1:15 4 x 75 (Free/NonFree/Free) @ 1:15 4 x 25 Breast @ :45

SPRINT	5 x {
	   200 Best Average @ 3:00
	   4 x 50 Best Avg. @ :50 + 1:00 rest
	}

DISTANCE	4 x (200 + 100 easy) D 1-4 4 x (75 + 25 easy) All Red 8 x (50 + 50 easy) D 1-4 , D 5-8 to MAX

MID-DISTANCE	5 x {
	   400 @ 4:30/4:45/4:50
	   4 x 100 Goal 500 Pace @ 1:10/1:15/1:20
	   1:00 rest
	}

WEEK 13	Tue Nov 21 2023
WARMUP	3 x 200 #1 Free #2 (50 BK/50 Breast) #3 DPS Choice 3 x 100 Non-Free work walls @ 1:40 6 x 50 Fist Drill @ 1:00 6 x 25 Build @ :30 12 x 25 @ :30 underwater kick w/fins (1:00) 4 x 50 Dolphin on back w/fins @ :45 (:30) 4 x 50 Dolphin on back w/fins @ :40
MAIN SET	1 x 400 Free @ 4:50 2 x 50 Hold Goal 200 Pace @ 1:00 1 x 400 Free @ 5:00 2 x 50 Hold Goal 200 Pace @ 1:00 1 x 400 Free @ 5:10 2 x 50 Hold Goal 200 Pace @ 1:00

WEEK 13	Wed Nov 22 2023
WARMUP	1 x 500 (200 Free/200 Non-Free/100 RIMO) 8 x 100 @ :10 rest odds: #1 Stroke (50 drill/50 swim) evens: (50 Bk/50 BR) 8 x 100 (25 Build/50 Pink/25 Build to Fast Finish) @ 1:40 8 x 50 @ 1:00 #1-3 (1/2 underwater Kick + breakout on each wall) #4-6 Build max of 3 breaths #7-8 DPS
SPRINT	6 x 75 Build @ 1:15 1 x 400 pull @ 5:00 5 x 100 (3) White (2) Pink @ 1:30 1 x 300 (150 Kick no board / 150 Swim) @ 5:30 5 x 50 (3) White (1) Pink (1) Red @ 1:00

DISTANCE	4 x 50 #1 drill, #2 build, #3 drill, #4 sprint @ :30
	2 x {
	1 x 100 @ 7:00
	4 x 50 @ 4:00
	}
	1 x 400 White
	10 x 100 (50 kick/50 swim) @ 1:40
	8 x 50 Non-Free @ :50

MID-DISTANCE	6 x 100 @ 1:30 1 x 400 DPS @ 5:00 8 x 50 (2 white/ 2 pink/ 2 red/ 2 pink) @ :50 (:30) 1 x 400 DPS @ 5:00 5 x 100 blue @ 1:20 (:30) 1 x 300 Negative Split @ 4:00 8 x 25 Build to MAX finish @ :30

WEEK 13	Thu Nov 23 2023
WARMUP	1 x 400 (200 Free/200 Back) 1 x 300 (150 Kick non-free/150 kick breast) 1 x 200 (100 BK/100 Choice) 1 x 100 IM 6 x 150 Kick w/fins @ 1:45 (1:00) 8 x 50 Kick no board @ 1:00 D1-4,5-8
MAIN SET	4 x 100 MAX 4 x 50 MAX 4 x 50 MAX 12 x 50 (50 Kick/50 Swim) 4 x 100 JMI

WEEK 13	Fri Nov 24 2023
WARMUP	1 x 500 (200 Free/200 Non-Free/100 RIMO) 8 x 100 @ :10 rest odds: # 1 Stroke (50 drill/50 swim) evens: (50 Bk/50 BR) 10 x 100 @ 1:30 odds: (25 kick/25 drill/50 swim with no breath turns) evens: DPS
SPRINT	2 x 300 DPS @ 4:00 5 x 100 (3) White (2) Pink @ 1:30 1 x 300 (150 Kick no board/ 150 Swim) @ 5:30 5 x 100 (3) White (1) Pink (1) Red @ 1:30
DISTANCE	4 x 200 Pull - Kick - Pink - White 2 x 800 odd 100's: Descend even 100's Kick Pink 6 x 200 odds: Blue @ 2:20 evens: IM @ 2:40 5 x 100's (100's Descend 1-5 Red + 25 MAX)
MID-DISTANCE	5 x 100 Negative Split (50 White/50 Red) @ 1:20 1 x Broken 500 @ 100s : 10 seconds 1 x 500 (200 White/300 Pink) @ 6:30/6:45 8 x 100 (alternate free/non-free) @ 1:30 1 x 300 blue @ 4:50/5:10 6 x 100 (back/free/choice/fly) @ +:10 8 x 50 Hold 1650 Goal Pace @ :50

WEEK 13	Sat Nov 25 2023
WARMUP	3 x 300 Paddle/Pull @ 3:45/4:00 BP - 5 3 x 300 @ 3:45/3:55 (1:00) 8 x 25 Paddles DPS – Count Stroke per 25 @ :45 4 x 25 Keep Same Stroke Count as w/ paddles per 25 5 x 50 drill @ 1:00 4 x 25 Kick Build each 25 @ :40 4 x 50 Kick Descend @ :55 4 x 25 Kick @ :30 9 x 50 (2 @ :40, 1 @ :30)

MAIN SET	2 x 300 (200 Free/100 IM)
	1 x 300 Kick no board
	8 x 75 -2 of each Stroke kick/drill/swim by 25s @ 1:30
	
	5 x 200 Pull @ 2:40/2:45
	odds: BP: 3
	evens: BP: 5
	
	1 x 200 kick no board @ 3:30
	4 x 75 @ 1:20
	   odds: white/pink/red
	   evens:red/pink/white
	
	2 x {
	1 x 400 w/fins @ 5:00
	4 x 50 kick dolphin on back @ :45
	}
	16 x 25 w/fins underwater kick @ :50
	8 x 75 w/ chutes @ 1:20

NOVEMBER- DECEMBER   ELITE SWIM WORKOUT '24   WEEK 14

Monday	Tuesday	Wednesday	Thursday	Friday	Saturday
500 SKIMPS 4 x 100 IM @ 1:20/1:40 6 x 75 (Kick/drill/swim) @ 1:10 8 x 25 @ :30 odds: drill/ evens: Stroke SPRINT 6 x 50 @ 5:00 #1-2 MAX 2 Breaths TOTAL #3-4 MAX 1 Breath TOTAL #5-6 MAX 0 Breath TOTAL 4 x 50 MAX w/ fins from dive 1 x 50 w/ fins from push DISTANCE 4 x 200 w/ fins @ 2:40/2:50 (:30) 4 x 200 IM @ 3:30 4 x 50 @ 1:30 No breath into and out of each turn 4 x 25 MAX breakout @ :30 10 x 50 MAX @ 4:00 MID-DISTANCE 2 x 600 @ 7:50 Odd 200s - DPS 8 x 100 D1-6 , Hold time on 7-8 @ 1:30 (2:00) 6 x 75 w/chutes @ 1:20 D1-3, 4-6 2 x 400 @ 5:00/5:10 4 x 100 JMI @ 1:05/1:10 (1:00) 8 x 50 Hold 500 Goal Pace or 200 Goal Pace + 2 @ 1:00	1 x 300 Free 2 x 200 (100 Kick/100 Swim Non-Free) 8 x 50 @ 1:00 odds: fast turns evens: build to fast finish Free 12 x 100 odds: RB5 @ 1:40 evens: RB6 @ 1:30 2 x 800 @ :30 rest #1 Negative Split #2 Ascend 8 x 100 JMI @ 1:05/1:10	1 x 200 Kick no board 3 x 100 BackStroke 1 x 200 Kick with board 3 x 100 Freestyle 3 x (1 x 300 Paddle w/Pull Buoy @ 4:00 3 x 100 Pull @ 1:30) 8 x 25 w/fins underwater kick @ :30 4 x 50 w/fins underwater kick @ 1:00 (Max of 1 breath allowed per 50) SPRINT 50 Pink 100 (Pink 50 x 2) @ 2:20/2:30 200 (100 max + Pink 50 x 2) @ 4:00/4:30 300 (200 max + Pink 50 x 2) @ 5:20/6:00 50 Red 100 (Red 50 x 2) @ 2:20/2:30 200 (100 max + Red 50 x 2) @ 4:00/4:30 300 (200 max + Red 50 x 2) @ 5:20/6:00 DISTANCE 3 x 200 @ 2:50 3 x 400 Clear-White-Pink @ 5:50 3 x 300 White-Pink-Red @ 4:50 3 x 200 Pink-Red-Blue @ 3:50 3 x 100 Red-Blue-MAX@ 1:30 MID-DISTANCE 3 x 1650s (pink - red - max)	100 SKIMPS 3 x 100 IM-Choice-NonFree 4 x 100 @ 125 8 x 50 @ 1:00 9 x 100 #1-3 D1-3 to Pink #4-6 Bp 5/7 by 50 #7-9 Build each turn to MAX flip + 3 MAX Strokes Breakout 3 x 100 (white/pink/red) @ 1:50 2 x 100 red – blue @ 1:30 4 x 50 D 1-4 @ 1:10 6 x 25 Dive –max finish 4 x 200 (free/stroke/kick) @ 3:00	3 x 500 #1 IM #2 IM #3 Choice Swim 1 x 300 Kick w/ fins no board @ 4:10/4:20 4 x 50 Fast kick Flutter @ :40/:45 1 x 300 Kick w/ fins no board @ 4:00/4:10 4 x 50 Fast kick Dolphin @ :40/:45 SPRINT 4 x 100 IM @ 1:50 4 x 50 Build/MAX finish last 12.5 @ 1:00 4 x 100 IM @ 1:50 4 x 50 Build/MAX last 25 @ 1:00 4 x 100 JMI @ 1:00/1:05 (2:00) 4 x 50 @ :30/:35 10 x 50 @ 1:00 Odds 50 Kick Evens 50 Swim DISTANCE 5 x 100 Paddle/Pull @ 1:20/1:30 4 x (200 + 100 easy) (2:00) 8 x (75 + 25 easy) White-Pink-Red-White x 2 2 x (50 + 50 easy) Hold 200 Goal Pace +1 MID-DISTANCE 3 x (500 + 100 easy) #1 White #2 Build each 100 #3 Pink 6 x (200 + 50 easy) #1-2 IM Swim #3-4 Kick Red #5-6 Swim Red 10 x (100 + 50 easy) #1-5 Hold 1000 Goal Pace +3 #6-8 Hold 1000 Goal Pace +2 #9-10 Hold 1000 Goal Pace +1	600 (300 Free/300 Non-Free) 400 Free 200 Kick 200 (100 BK/50 Choice/50 Kick) 12 x 75 @ 1:10 Fly-Back-Breast/Back-Breast-Free 6 x 100 IM @ 1:50 8 x 50 IMO @ 1:00 1 x 600 Free 1 x 400 RIMO drill/swim 1 x 200 Non-Free 8 x 50 2 each Stroke drill/swim @ :10 rest 1 x 600 Paddle/Pull 1 x 200 choice 6 x 100 @ 1:10/1:15 Keep all the same speed

WEEK 14	Mon Nov 27 2023
WARMUP	500 SKIMPS 4 x 100 IM @ 1:20/1:40 6 x 75 (Kick/drill/swim) @ 1:10 8 x 25 @ :30 odds: drill/ evens: Stroke
SPRINT	6 x 50 @ 6:00 #1-2 MAX 2 Breaths TOTAL #3-4 MAX 1 Breath TOTAL #5-6 MAX 0 Breath TOTAL 4 x 50 MAX w/ fins from dive 1 x 50 w/ fins from push
DISTANCE	4 x 200 w/ fins @ 2:40/2:50 (:30) 4 x 200 IM @ 3:30 4 x 50 @ 1:30 No breath into and out of each turn 4 x 25 MAX breakout @ :30 10 x 50 MAX @ 4:00
MID-DISTANCE	2 x 600 @ 7:50 Odd 200s - DPS 8 x 100 D 1-6 , Hold time on 7-8 @ 1:30 (2:00) 6 x 75 w/ chutes @ 1:20 D1-3, 4-6 2 x 400 @ 5:00/5:10 4 x 100 JMI @ 1:05/1:10 (1:00) 8 x 50 Hold 500 Goal Pace or 200 Goal Pace + 2 @ 1:00

WEEK 14	Tue Nov 28 2023
WARMUP	1 x 300 Free 2 x 200 (100 Kick / 100 Swim Non-Free) 8 x 50 @ 1:00 odds: fast turns evens: build to fast finish
MAIN SET	12 x 100 Free odds: RB5 @ 1:40 evens: RB6 @ 1:30 2 x 800 @ :30 rest #1 Negative Split #2 Ascend 8 x 100 JMI @ 1:05 / 1:10

WEEK 14	Wed Nov 29 2023

WARMUP	1 x 200 Kick no board
	3 x 100 BackStroke
	1 x 200 Kick with board
	3 x 100 Freestyle
	3 x {
	   1 x 300 Paddle w/Pull Buoy @ 4:00
	   3 x 100 Pull @ 1:30
	}
	8 x 25 w/fins underwater kick @ :30
	4 x 50 w/fins underwater kick @ 1:00
	(Max of 1 breath allowed per 50)

SPRINT	50 Pink 100 (Pink 50 x 2) @ 2:20/2:30 200 (100 max + Pink 50 x 2) @ 4:00/4:30 300 (200 max + Pink 50 x 2) @ 5:20/6:00 50 Red 100 (Red 50 x 2) @ 2:20/2:30 200 (100 max + Red 50 x 2 @ 4:00/4:30 300 (200 max + Red 50 x 2) @ 5:20/6:00
DISTANCE	3 x 200 @ 2:50 3 x 400 Clear-White-Pink @ 5:50 3 x 300 White-Pink-Red @ 4:50 3 x 200 Pink-Red-Blue @ 3:50 3 x 100 Red-Blue-MAX@ 1:30
MID-DISTANCE	3 x 1650s (pink - red - max)

WEEK 14	Thu Nov 30 2023
WARMUP	100 SKIMPS 3 x 100 IM-Choice-NonFree 4 x 100 @ 1:25 8 x 50 @ 1:00 9 x 100 #1-3 D1-3 to Pink #4-6 Bp 5/7 by 50 #7-9 Build each turn to MAX flip + 3 MAX Strokes Breakout
MAIN SET	3 x 100 (white/pink/red) @ 1:50 2 x 100 red – blue @ 1:30 4 x 50 D 1-4 @ 1:10 6 x 25 Dive -max finish 4 x 200 (free/stroke/kick) @ 3:00

WEEK 14	Fri Dec 01 2023
WARMUP	3 x 500 #1 IM #2 IM #3 Choice Swim 1 x 300 Kick w/ fins no board @ 4:10/4:20 4 x 50 Fast kick Flutter @ :1:00 1 x 300 Kick w/ fins no board @ 4:00/4:10 4 x 50 Fast kick Dolphin w/fins @ :45
SPRINT	4 x 100 IM @ 1:50 4 x 50 Build/MAX finish last 12.5 @ 1:00 4 x 100 IM @ 1:50 4 x 50 Build/MAX last 25 @ 1:00 4 x 100 JMI @ 1:00/1:05 (2:00) 4 x 50 @ :30/:35 10 x 50 @ 1:00 Odds 50 Kick Evens 50 Swim
DISTANCE	5 x 100 Paddle/Pull @ 1:20/1:30 4 x (200 + 100 easy) (2:00) 8 x (75 + 25 easy) White-Pink-Red-White x 2 2 x (50 + 50 easy) Hold 200 Goal Pace + 1
MID-DISTANCE	3 x (500 + 100 easy) #1 White #2 Build each 100 #3 Pink 6 x (200 + 50 easy) #1-2 IM Swim #3-4 Kick Red #5-6 Swim Red 10 x (100 + 50 easy) #1-5 Hold 1000 Goal Pace +3 #6-8 Hold 1000 Goal Pace +2 #9-10 Hold 1000 Goal Pace +1

WEEK 14	Sat Dec 02 2023
WARMUP	600 (300 Free/300 Non-Free) 400 Free 200 Kick 200 (100 BK/50 Choice/50 kick) 12 x 75 @ 1:10 Fly-Back-Breast/Back-Breast-Free 6 x 100 IM @ 1:50 8 x 50 IMO @ 1:00
MAIN SET	1 x 600 Free 1 x 400 RIMO drill/swim 1 x 200 Non-Free 8 x 50 2 each Stroke drill/swim @ :10 rest 1 x 600 Paddle/Pull 1 x 200 choice 6 x 100 @ 1:10/1:15 Keep all the same speed

DECEMBER   ELITE SWIM WORKOUT '24   WEEK 15

Monday	Tuesday	Wednesday	Thursday	Friday	Saturday
6 x 150 odds: Free evens: (50 Back/50 BR/50 Choice) 4 x 75 #1-4 IMO Kick (Kick/Swim) @ 1:00	1 x 400 Free 1 x 200 Kick with board 3 x 100 Freestyle	1 x 300 Free 2 x 100 BackStroke 1 x 200 Free 2 x 100 Back	500 Free 6 x 100 IM @ :15 rest 4 x 100 Kick IM Order	1 x 300 Free 2 x 200 #1 Kick no board, #2 Kick Board 5 x 100 odds: IM, evens: Choice	400 IM 8 x 50 Kick @ :10 rest 10 x 100 @ :15 rest Odds: Back Evens: Free

5 x 100 @ 1:30
#1-2 Max of 2 breaths each 25
#3-4 (50 Free/50 Back)
#5 Max of 2 breaths each 25
	4 x 200 Kick @ 4:00
	50 Kick Pink/50 Kick Red/50 Kick Pink/50 Kick Red
	100 Kick Pink/100 Kick Red
	100 Kick Red/100 Kick Pink
	50 Kick Red/50 Kick Pink/50 Kick Red/50 Kick Pink
		2 x {
		4 x 25 fist drill
		2 x 25 Stroke build
		}
		4 x 25 (drill/build/drill/sprint) @ :40
			6 x 75 w/fins (drill/swim/drill) @ 1:10
			6 x 75 w/fins (underwater kick/swim/dolphin on back) @ 1:15
				6 x 200
				#1-2 (100 Back/100 Breast) @ +:20 rest
				#3-4 Choice Swim @ 2:40
				#5-6 (50 BK/100 Kick no board/50 Choice)
					1 x 400 (100 Free/100 Non-Free/100 Kick no board/100 Free/100 Non Free)
					8 x 75 (Free/Non-Free/Drill) @ 1:10

SPRINT
1 x 300 FR/Non-FR by 50
3 x 100 IM (2) Pink (1) Red @ 1:10
4 x 50 JMI @ :40/:45
(2:00)
1 x 200 FR/Non-FR by 100
2 x 100 JMI Red-Blue @ 1:50
4 x 50 JMI Dolphin kick @ :55/1:00
(1:00)
1 x 100 FR Blue
1 x 100 IM White @ 1:50
4 x 50 1 Breath @ 1:20
	SPRINT
	1 x 300 White @ 4:00
	4 x 50 D 1-4 @ 1:00
	4 x 100 White @ 1:40
	4 x 50 D 1-4 @ 1:00
	200 White
	4 x 50 Max Breakout @ 1:30
		SPRINT
		8 x 100 White @ 1:20
		4 x 50 @ :40
		6 x 100 IM @ 1:30
		4 x 50 @ :40
		
		2 x {
		1 x 200 @ 2:30
		4 x 50 @ 1:00
		Descend Descend
		}
		1 x 50 w/fins from push, MAX
			1 x 800 Descend the 200's 1-4 (:30 rest)
			2 x 600 White-Pink @ 7:30/7:45 (:30 rest)
			1 x 500 (100 Pink/200 Red/100 Blue/100 MAX)
				SPRINT
				1 x 200 Paddle Pull Descend each 50 @ 4:00
				4 x 50 25 MAX underwater kick/ 25 white @ 1:00
				4 x 25 (12.5 MAX kick/12.5 white) @ :30
				8 x 50 MAX @ 5:00
				
				1 x 600
				odd 100's: back
				even 100's: (50 breast kick on back/50 free)
					1 x 400 Kick

DISTANCE 4 x 300 w/ fins @ 3:40/3:50 (:30) 4 x 100 IM @ 1:30 4 x 50 @ 1:00 No breath into and out of each turn 4 x 25 MAX breakout @ :30 10 x 50 MAX @ 4:00		**DISTANCE** 1 x 50 MAX from Dive @ :30 1 x 200 JMI @ 2:05 1 x 25 MAX underwater kick from Dive @ :40 1 x 200 MAX for time	8 x 75 Chutes @ 1:30 25 no breath/50 Build	**DISTANCE** 2 x 400 (200 White Free/200 Pink BK) @ 5:30/5:40 4 x 100 IM @ 1:30/1:50 5 x 50 drill @ 1:00 (1:00) 3 x 200 Fin Swim @ 2:15/2:20 6 x 50 w/fins under/over @ 1:00	5 x 100 @ 1:15/1:25 Keep all the same speed 1 x 200 Pink
MID-DISTANCE 4 x 200 @ + :20 #1 Free #2 Non-Free #3 back/Kick by 50's #4 IM (1:00) 12 x 50 #1-6 Neg Split (Clear/Pink) @ :45 #7-12 No Breath off walls for 3 Strokes @ :45		**MID-DISTANCE** 3 x 600 Paddle w/Pull Buoy #1 Descend each 100 #2 Descend each 200 #3 Descend each 300 to MAX		6 x 100 odds: JMI Free @ 1:10/1:15 evens: IM @ 1:15/1:20	
4 x 100 @ +:10 #1 Free #2 Past flags on each wall choice #3 Non-Free #4 Drill (1:00) 6 x 100 #1-3 D1-3 #4-6 Fast breakout on each wall		8 x (150 + 50 easy) odds: Free evens: Non-Free Pink 8 x 50 Dolphin on Back @ 1:00		**MID-DISTANCE** 1 x (600 + 200 easy) Pink 4 x (300 + 100) D 1-4 to Pink 4 x (200 + 50 easy) White-Pink-Red-Red 8 x (100 + 50 easy) All Red 8 x (50 + 50 easy) Hold Goal 1000 Pace	
8 x 50 w/fins (25 underwater/25 swim) @ 1:10		10 (100 + 100 easy) 500 (75 Free/25 Breast)			
2 x 400 Fin Swim #1 Free #2 IM		10 x 75 (25 Kick Streamline/25 Fist/25 Build) @ 1:15			
		6 x 125 (25 Dolphin Kick on back/75 Back/25 underwater) @ 2:00			

WEEK 15	Mon Dec 04 2023
WARMUP	6 x 150 odds: Free evens: (50 Back/50 BR/50 Choice) 4 x 75 #1-4 IMO (Kick/Swim) @ 1:00 5 x 100 @ 1:30 #1-2 Max of 2 breaths each 25 #3-4 (50 Free/50 Back) #5 Max of 2 breaths each 25
SPRINT	1 x 300 FR/Non-FR by 50 3 x 100 IM (2) Pink (1) Red @ 1:20 4 x 50 JMI @ :45 (2:00) 1 x 200 FR/Non-FR by 100 2 x 100 JMI Red-Blue @ 1:50 4 x 50 JMI Dolphin kick @ 1:00 (1:00) 1 x 100 FR Blue 1 x 100 IM White @ 1:50 4 x 50- 1 Breath @ 1:40
DISTANCE	4 x 300 w/ fins @ 3:40/3:50 (:30) 4 x 100 IM @ 1:30 4 x 50 @ 1:00 No breath into and out of each turn 4 x 25 MAX breakout @ :30 10 x 50 MAX @ 4:00
MID-DISTANCE	4 x 200 @ + :20 #1 Free #2 Non-Free #3 back/Kick by 50's #4 IM (1:00) 12 x 50 #1-6 Neg Split (Clear/Pink) @ :45 #7-12 No Breath off walls for 3 Strokes @ :45 4 x 100 @ + :10 #1 Free #2 Past flags on each wall choice #3 Non-Free #4 Drill (1:00) 6 x 100 #1-3 D1-3 #4-6 Fast breakout on each wall 8 x 50 w/fins (25 underwater/25 swim) @ 1:10 2 x 400 Fin Swim #1 Free #2 IM

WEEK 15	Tue Dec 05 2023
WARMUP	1 x 400 Free 1 x 200 Kick with board 3 x 100 Freestyle 4 x 200 Kick @ 4:00 50 Kick Pink/50 Kick Red/50 Kick Pink/50 Kick Red 100 Kick Pink/100 Kick Red 100 Kick Red/100 Kick Pink 50 Kick Red/50 Kick Pink/50 Kick Red/50 Kick Pink
MAIN SET	1 x 300 White @ 4:00 4 x 50 D 1-4 @ 1:00 4 x 100 White @ 1:40 4 x 50 D 1-4 @ 1:00 200 White 4 x 50 Max Breakout@ 1:30

WEEK 15	Wed Dec 06 2023

WARMUP	1 x 300 Free
	2 x 100 BackStroke
	1 x 200 Free
	2 x 100 Back
	2 x {
	    4 x 25 fist drill
	    2 x 25 Stroke build
	}
	4x 25 (drill/build/drill/sprint) @ :40

SPRINT	8 x 100 White @ 1:20
	4 x 50 @ :40
	6 x 100 IM @ 1:30
	4 x 50 @ :40
	2 x {
	    1 x 200 @ 2:30
	    4 x 50 @ 1:00
	    Descend Descend
	}
	1 x 50 w/fins from push, MAX

DISTANCE	1 x 50 MAX from Dive @ :30 1 x 200 JMI @ 2:05 1 x 25 MAX underwater kick from Dive @ :40 1 x 200 MAX for time
MID-DISTANCE	3 x 600 Paddle w/Pull Buoy #1 Descend each 100 #2 Descend each 200 #3 Descend each 300 to MAX 8 x (150 + 50 easy) odds: Free evens: Non-Free Pink 8 x 50 Dolphin on Back @ 1:00 10 x (100 + 100 easy) 500 (75 Free/25 Breast) 10 x 75 (25 Kick Streamline/25 Fist/25 Build) @ 1:15 6 x 125 (25 Dolphin Kick on back/75 Back/25 underwater) @ 2:00

WEEK 15	Thu Dec 07 2023
WARMUP	500 Free 6 x 100 IM @ :15 rest 4 x 100 Kick IM Order 6 x 75 w/fins (drill/swim/drill) @ 1:10 6 x 75 w/fins (underwater kick/swim/dolphin on back) @ 1:15
MAIN SET	1 x 800 Descend the 200's 1-4 (:30 rest) 2 x 600 White-Pink @ 7:30/7:45 (:30 rest) 1 x 500 (100 Pink/200 Red/100 Blue/100 MAX) 8 x 75 Chutes @ 1:30 25 no breath/50 Build

WEEK 15	Fri Dec 08 2023
WARMUP	1 x 300 Free 2 x 200 #1 Kick no board, #2 Kick Board 5 x 100 odds: IM, evens: Choice 6 x 200 #1-2 (100 Back / 100 Breast) @ +:20 rest #3-4 Choice Swim @ 2:40 #5-6 (50 BK / 100 Kick no board / 50 Choice)
SPRINT	1 x 200 Paddle Pull Descend each 50 @ 4:00 4 x 50 25 MAX underwater kick / 25 white @ 1:00 4 x 25 (12.5 MAX kick / 12.5 white) @ :30 8 x 50 MAX @ 5:00 1 x 600 odd 100's: back even 100's: (50 breast kick on back / 50 free)
DISTANCE	2 x 400 (200 White Free / 200 Pink BK) @ 5:30 / 5:40 4 x 100 IM @ 1:30 / 1:50 5 x 50 drill @ 1:00 (1:00) 3 x 200 Fin Swim @ 2:15 / 2:20 6 x 50 w/ fins under / over @ 1:00 6 x 100 odds: JMI Free @ 1:10 / 1:15 evens: IM @ 1:15 / 1:20
MID-DISTANCE	1 x (600 + 200 easy) Pink 4 x (300 + 100) D 1-4 to Pink 4 x (200 + 50 easy) White-Pink-Red-Red 8 x (100 + 50 easy) All Red 8 x (50 + 50 easy) Hold Goal 1000 Pace

WEEK 15	Sat Dec 09 2023
WARMUP	400 IM 8 x 50 Kick @ :10 rest 10 x 100 @ :15 rest Odds: Back Evens: Free 1 x 400 (100 Free / 100 Non-Free / 100 Kick no board / 100 Free / 100 Non Free) 8 x 75 (Free / Non-Free / Drill) @ 1:10
MAIN SET	1 x 400 Kick 5 x 100 @ 1:15 / 1:25 Keep all the same speed 1 x 200 Pink

Monday

200 SKIMPS
Pull: (2 x 25 Choice/75 Swim)

8 x 75 @ 1:30
odds: Free drill
evens: Non-Free drill

2 x 8 x 50 (25 Drill/ 25 build to max finish) @ :50
6 x 100 Kick w/fins @ 1:20/1:30
25 underwater kick/25 dolphin on back/50 kick choice

SPRINT

4 x 200 DPS @ 3:50
4 x 50 Non-Free @ :55

4 x 200 IM @ 3:00
5 x 100 IM @ 1:30

8 x 100 @ 1:40
odds: Red Choice
evens: 50 RB: 4/50 white

4 x 25's Max start + breakout, white finish

DISTANCE

8 x 50 (25 Drill/ 25 build to max finish) @ :50
6 x 75 @ 5:00 MAX
4 x 50 @ 4:00 MAX
1 x 400 (Non-Free/Choice/BK/Choice)

MID-DISTANCE

2 x 400 White/Pink @ 4:00
4 x 100 D 1-4 @ 1:30
600 White
3 x 100 Work the Turns @ 1:30
2 x 300 Pink/Red @ 3:50
300 Negative Split

4 x 50 Build to great finish @ 1:00

Tuesday

400 IM
8 x 50 Kick @ :10 rest
10 x 100 @ :15 rest
Odds: Breast
Evens: Free

4 x 75
Each 25 - 12.5 underwater kick/12.5 swim
4 x 25 underwater Kick @ :40

2 x 500 Paddle/Fins @ 6:00/6:30
#1 Build each 100 to MAX flip + 5 Strokes MAX no breath
#2 Descend 100's

5 x (200 IM Best Average @ 2:20/2:40/2:50 + 4 x 50 IMO Avg B.T. 200 Pace - 1 + 1:00 rest)

Wednesday

8 x 100 @ 1:30
odds: Free
evens: (50 Fly drill/50 Choice)

4 x 75 (25 fist drill/25 swim/25 build) @ 1:20
8 x 50 (25 kick no board/25 swim) @ 1:00

SPRINT

4 x 25 MAX
8 x 100 Best Average @ 1:20
1 x 300 white
2x(5 x 50 D1-5 to MAX) 10
5 x 200 Best Average @ 2:40

DISTANCE

1 x 400 easy Kick
8 x 50 Kick
#1-4 Descend to Pink
#5-8 Dolphin on back all Red

4 x 300 DPS @ 3:40/3:50/4:00
8 x 50 Non-Free @ :50

4 x 200 IM @ 2:30/2:40/2:50
8 x (50 IMO + choice 50) @ 1:30
Pink IMO

8 x 100 @ 1:40
odds: 50 kick/50 swim
evens: 50 swim max of 5 breaths

MID-DISTANCE

1 x 1200 (300 White/300 Pink/300 Red/300 Pink)

4 x 100 JMI @ 1:05/1:10
1 x 800 (200 White/200 Pink/(:30)/200 Red/200 Pink) (:30)

4 x 100 JMI @ 1:05/1:15
1 x 600 (200 White/200 Pink/200 Red) (2:00)
5 x 100 Best Average @ 1:20/1:30

Thursday

1000 Choice white
10 x 50 Kick D 1-4, 5-10 White

1 x 600 Paddle/Pull
Bp 5 by 100's work on great turns
1 x 400

IM
8 x 100 Build
#1-4 IMO w/fins @ 1:20/1:30
#5-8 IM 1:30/1:40

2 x (
1 x 100 Back JMI @ 1:20/1:30
4 x 25 Back 15m underwater @ :20
1 x 100 Breast RED @ 1:50
4 x 25 Free JMI (max of 3 breaths) @ :30
1 x 100 Free MAX @ 4:00
}
8 x 50 Kick w/chutes IMO @ 1:20

Friday

500 Free
200 Back

3 x200
#1 Free
#2 (Back/Breast by 50's)
#3 (100 Choice/100 IM)

2 x 100 Paddle w/Pull Buoy @ 2:30/2:40
4 x 100 Pull @ 1:30

4 x 75 Stroke (long underwater on each wall) @ 1:20
4 x 50 25 build to top speed, 25 easy @ 1:00

SPRINT

8 x 25 (Max 12.5/ white 12.5) :10 sec
6 x 50 @ 3:30
#1-2 Three Breaths
#3 Two Breaths
#5 One Breath
#6 No Breath
8 x 50 Kick MAX @ 1:00
10 x 100 @ 1:05/1:15 JMI

DISTANCE

1 x 600 Free
1 x 400 IM
8 x 50 IMO x 2 @ :10 rest

6 x 150 (Drill/Kick/Swim) @ 2:15
5 x 50 fist #1 Stroke @ 1:00
4 x 25 build to pink @ :30

1 x 400 IM @ 5:10/5:30/6:00/6:30
4 x 50 Kick no board IMO @ :45/:50
4 x 200 IM @ 3:00/3:15/3:30/3:40
8 x 50 kick no board #1 Stroke @ :50

8 x 50 Chutes @ 1:15/1:20
10 x 50 w/ fins (12.5 underwater kick/12.5 swim) @ 1:00

MID-DISTANCE

2 x 600 (300 White/300 Kick Red) @ 10:30/10:50
3 x 300 (150 Pink/150 Red Kick) @ 8:40/8:50
10 x 100 D1-5 , Hold time on 5-8, 9-10 MAX

1 x 300 JMI @ 4:00/4:20
2 x 200 JMI @ 4:00/4:20
#1 Flutter #2 Dolphin
4 x 50 Red Swim @ 1:10/1:15

Saturday

200 SKIMPS

8 x 50 Drill @ 1:20
odds: 25 Left Arm Free/25 Right Arm Free
evens: 25 Catchup/25 Stroke

50 Kick @ :10 rest
100 Free @ :10 rest
200 non-Free @ :10 rest
300 Kick @ :10 rest
200 Fin Swim @ :10 rest
100 Free @ :10 rest
50 Worst Stroke @ :10 rest

SPRINT

3 x (100 Red from Blocks
200 white
100 MAX from push
100 white

1 x 400 (100 Free/100 Back)
2 x 200 (Choice drill)

2 x (
1 x 25 MAX from Dive @ :30
1 x 75 JMI @ 1:10/1:15
1 x 50 kick ½ way underwater on every wall @ :40/:45
1 x 25 MAX underwater kick from Dive @ :40
}
1 x 100 MAX for time

Cooldown
3 x 200 choice 3:00

WEEK 16	Mon Dec 11 2023
WARMUP	200 SKIMPS Pull- (2 x 25 Choice / 75 Swim) 8 x 75 @ 1:30 odds: Free drill evens: Non-Free drill 2 x 8 x 50 (25 Drill/ 25 build to max finish) @ :50 6 x 100 Kick w/fins @ 1:20/1:30 25 underwater kick/25 dolphin on back/50 kick choice

SPRINT	4 x 200 DPS @ 3:50
	4 x 50 Non-Free @ :55
	4 x 200 IM @ 3:00
	5 x 100 IM @ 1:30
	8 x 100 @ 1:40
	   odds: Red Choice
	   evens: 50 RB: 4/50 white
	
	4 x 25's Max start + breakout, white finish

DISTANCE	8 x 50 (25 Drill/ 25 build to max finish) @ :50 6 x 75 @ 5:00 MAX 4 x 50 @ 4:00 MAX 1 x 400 (Non-Free/Choice/BK/Choice)
MID-DISTANCE	2 x 400 White/Pink @ 4:00 4 x 100 D 1-4 @ 1:30 600 White 3 x 100 Work the Turns @ 1:30 2 x 300 Pink/Red @ 3:50 300 Negative Split 4 x 50 Build to great finish @ 1:00

WEEK 16	Tue Dec 12 2023
WARMUP	400 IM 8 x 50 Kick @ :10 rest 10 x 100 @ :15 rest Odds: Breast Evens: Free 4 x 75 Each 25 - 12.5 underwater kick / 12.5 swim 4 x 25 underwater Kick @ :40 2 x 500 Paddle / Fins @ 6:00 / 6:30 #1 Build each 100 to MAX flip + 5 Strokes MAX no breath #2 Descend 100's
MAIN SET	5 x 200 IM Best Average @ 2:20 / 2:40 / 2:50 4 x 50 IMO Avg B.T. 200 Pace – 1 (1:00 rest)

WEEK 16	Wed Dec 13 2023
WARMUP	8 x 100 @ 1:30 odds: Free evens: (50 Fly drill/50 Choice) 4 x 75 (25 fist drill/25 swim/25 build) @ 1:20 8 x 50 (25 kick no board/25 swim) @ 1:00
SPRINT	4 x 25 MAX 8 x 100 Best Average @ 1:20 1 x 300 white 2x(5 x 50 D1-5 to MAX) :10 5 x 200 Best Average @ 2:40
DISTANCE	1 x 400 easy Kick 8 x 50 Kick #1-4 Descend to Pink #5-8 Dolphin on back all Red 4 x 300 DPS @ 3:40/3:50/4:00 8 x 50 Non-Free @ :50 4 x 200 IM @ 2:30/2:40/2:50 8 x (50 IMO + choice 50) @ 1:30 Pink IMO 8 x 100 @ 1:40 odds: 50 kick/50 swim evens: 50 swim max of 5 breaths
MID-DISTANCE	1 x 1200 (300 White/300 Pink/(:30)/300 Red/300 Pink) (:30) 4 x 100 JMI @ 1:05/1:10 1 x 800 (200 White/200 Pink/(:30)/200 Red/200 Pink) (:30) 4 x 100 JMI @ 1:05/1:15 1 x 600 (200 White/200 Pink/200 Red) (2:00) 5 x 100 Best Average @ 1:20/1:30

WEEK 16	Thu Dec 14 2023
WARMUP	1000 Choice white 10 x 50 Kick D 1-4, 5-10 White 1 x 600 Paddle/Pull Bp 5 by 100's work on great turns 1 x 400 IM 8 x 100 Build #1-4 IMO w/fins @ 1:20/1:30 #5-8 IM 1:30/1:40

MAIN SET	2 x {
	    1 x 100 Back JMI @ 1:20/1:30
	    4 x 25 Back 15m underwater @ :20
	    1 x 100 Breast RED @ 1:50
	    4 x 25 Free JMI (max of 3 breaths) @ :30
	    1 x 100 Free MAX @ 4:00
	}
	8 x 50 Kick w/chutes IMO @ 1:20

WEEK 16	Fri Dec 15 2023
WARMUP	500 Free 200 Back 3 x200 #1 Free #2 (Back/Breast by 50's) #3 (100 Choice/100 IM) 2 x 100 Paddle w/Pull Buoy @ 2:30/2:40 4 x 100 Pull @ 1:30 4 x 75 Stroke (long underwater on each wall) @ 1:20 4 x 50 25 build to top speed, 25 easy @ 1:00
SPRINT	8 x 25 (Max 12.5/ white 12.5) :10 sec 6 x 50 @ 3:30 #1-2 Three Breaths #3 Two Breaths #5 One Breath #6 No Breath 8 x 50 Kick MAX @ 1:00 10 x 100 @ 1:05/1:15 JMI
DISTANCE	1 x 600 Free 1 x 400 IM 8 x 50 IMO x 2 @ :10 rest 6 x 150 (Drill/Kick/Swim) @ 2:15 5 x 50 fist #1 Stroke @ 1:00 4 x 25 build to pink @ :30 1 x 400 IM @ 5:10/5:30/6:00/6:30 4 x 50 Kick no board IMO @ :45/:50 4 x 200 IM @ 3:00/3:15/3:30/3:40 8 x 50 kick no board #1 Stroke @ :50 8 x 50 Chutes @ 1:15/1:20 10 x 50 w/ fins (12.5 underwater kick/12.5 swim) @ 1:00
MID-DISTANCE	2 x 600 (300 White/300 Kick Red) @ 10:30/10:50 3 x 300 (150 Pink/150 Red Kick) @ 8:40/8:50 10 x 100 D1-5 , Hold time on 5-8, 9-10 MAX 1 x 300 JMI @ 4:00/4:20 2 x 200 Kick @ 4:00/4:20 #1 Flutter #2 Dolphin 4 x 50 Red Swim @ 1:10/1:15

WEEK 16	Sat Dec 16 2023
WARMUP	200 SKIMPS 8 x 50 Drill @ 1:20 odds: 25 Left Arm Free/25 Right Arm Free evens: 25 Catchup/25 Stroke 50 Kick @ :10 rest 100 Free @ :10 rest 200 non-Free @ :10 rest 300 Kick @ :10 rest 200 Fin Swim @ :10 rest 100 Free @ :10 rest 50 Worst Stroke @ :10 rest

MAIN SET	3 x { 100 Red from Blocks
	    200 white
	    100 MAX from push
	    100 white
	      }
	
	1 x 400 (100 Free/100 Back)
	2 x 200 (Choice drill)
	
	2 x {
	    1 x 25 MAX from Dive @ :30
	    1 x 75 JMI @ 1:10/1:15
	    1 x 50 kick ½ way underwater on every wall @ :40/:45
	    1 x 25 MAX underwater kick from Dive @ :40
	    1 x 100 MAX for time
	}
	Cooldown

Monday	Tuesday	Wednesday	Thursday	Friday	Saturday
1 x 600 Free 1 x 400 IM 1 x 200 Back 1 x 500 Kick 4 x 100 Kick (50 easy/50 Red) @ 2:00	2 x 300 #1 Free #2 RIMO (drill fly) 5 x 50 non-free @ :15 rest 5 x 100 Paddle w/Pull Buoy @ 1:30 6 x 50 Pull @ 1:00	1 x 600 (200 Free/200 BK/200 BR) 1 x 400 (200 Kick/200 Choice) 1 x 400 Paddle w/Pull Buoy DPS	6 x 50 drill/swim @ 1:00 1 x 600 Paddle/Pull Bp 5 by 100's work on great turns	400 RIMO 6 x 100 Non-Free (50 Kick/50 Swim) @ :10 rest 12 x 50 (4 x Fly/Free, Back/Free, Breast/Free) @ :10 rest	500 Free 200 Back 3 x200 #1 Free #2 (Back/Breast by 50's) #3 (100 Choice/100 IM)
8 x 50 IMO @ :50	2 x 100 Paddle w/Pull Buoy @ 2:30/2:40 4 x 100 Pull @ 1:30	4 x 100 IM (drill fly) @ 2:00/2:10 4 x 50 Back @ 1:00 6 x 50 (25 Breast Kick on Back) @ 1:10 4 x 75 (Free/NonFree/Free) @ 1:10 4 x 25 Breast @ :40	6 x 50 (25 fist/25 pink) @ 1:00 Concentrate on high elbow catch 6 x 50 Free Underwater Recovery Drill @ 1:00	16 x 50 @ :50 #1-4 sprint turns in & out of flags #5-8 BK 15 yds underwater kick + fast breakout #9-12 free with fast kick #13-16 Fly 25 kick/25 fast	4 x 50 choice @ 1:10
6 x 150 Fins / @ 1:30	4 x 75 Stroke (long underwater on each wall) @ 1:20 4 x 50 25 build to top speed, 25 easy @ 1:00	SPRINT 1 x 400 (200 White/200 Pink) 2 x 100 IM @ 2:00 10 x 50 @ 1:00 Odds 50 Free Evens 50 NonFree	1 x 400 Kick w/fins 5 x 50 Kick w/fins dolphin on back @ :50 6 x 25 underwater MAX kick w/fins @ :25	SPRINT 8 x 50 (25 Drill/ 25 build to max finish) @ :50	2 x 200 Scull #1 Front, #2 Back 4 x 50 Fist Drill @ 1:00 4 x 75 (fist drill/swim/build) @ 1:10

1 x 600 Kick @ 11:00
6 x 50 Kick D1-6 @ 1:00
1 x 100 MAX Kick
	2 x 500 Red
	2 x 300 Red (2:00)
	2 x 100 Red (2:00)
		2 x 200's MAX @ 2:30
		2 x 100's MAX @ 1:30
		4 x 50's MAX @ :50
		4 x 25's MAX @ :30
			8 x 25 IM @ :40	2 x 50 MAX
				6 x 25 work on breakout
					2 x {
					1 x 25 MAX from Dive @ :30
					1 x 100 JMI @ 1:15/1:25
					1 x 50 kick ½ way underwater on every wall @ :40/:45
					1 x 25 MAX underwater kick from Dive @ :40
					1 x 100 MAX for time
					}

SPRINT 6 x 150 Paddle/Pull @ 2:15	1 x 400 cool down	DISTANCE 2 x 200 Broken @ :50 6 x 50 Red @ 1:00	4 x (100 IMO + 50 white) @ 15 rest	4 x 50 D 1-4 @ 1:00 8 x 75 (free/kick/non-free) @ 1:20 6 x 150 (BK/Free/choice) @ :10 rest	
200 Kick		1 x 500 Free	3 x 300 @ :20 rest 5 x 100 IMO @ 1:50 #1-3: Descend #4-6: Descend to Max 5 x 100 JMI @ 1:10	DISTANCE 8 x 50 (25 Drill/ 25 build to max finish) @ :50 1 x Broken 200 @ 50 2 x Broken 100 @ 50 & 75 5 x 100 Kick @ 1:50 2 x 100 Pull @ 1:20 MID-DISTANCE	
6 x 25 Blue @ :30 10 x 25 Kick w/fins & chutes underwater @ 1:00		2 x 200 @ :20 rest #1 Choice #2 Non-Free		1 x 800 (200 Pull/ 200 Swim/ 200 Pull/ 200 IM) (1:00) 4 x 200 @ 2:20/2:30 Pink-Red-Blue-MAX	
DISTANCE 2 x 400 Paddle w/Pull Buoy @ 4:45/5:00 3 x 200 IM :30 sec 4 x 50 Free @ :40		MID-DISTANCE 8 x 100 IM pink @ 1:50		10 x 100 odds: Hold 500 goal pace @ 1:30 evens: White @ 1:35/1:40	

2 x 300 (150 Free/150 Non-Free) @
4 x 100 Descend @ 1:30
4 x 50 Free @ :40
		1 x Broken 1650
		1 x 500 Build @ :10 rest
		1 x 500 D 100s 1-5 @ :15 rest
		1 x 500 Red @ :20 rest
		1 x 100 Blue @ :10 rest
		1 x 50 MAX
				2 x {
				8 x 50 @ :45
				(:30)
				4 x 25 underwater @ :40
				}	

4 x 25's Max start + breakout MID-DISTANCE		1 x 800 White @ :20 rest 4 x 50 Kick @ 1:00			
3 x 500 max for time, from dive					

WEEK 17	Fri Dec 15 2023
WARMUP	1 x 600 Free 1 x 400 IM 1 x 200 Back 1 x 500 Kick 4 x 100 Kick (50 easy/50 Red) @ 2:00 8 x 50 IMO @ :50 6 x 150 Fins/ @ 1:30 1 x 600 Kick @ 11:00 6 x 50 Kick D1-6 @ 1:00 1 x 100 MAX Kick
SPRINT	6 x 150 Paddle/Pull @ 2:15 200 Kick 6 x 25 Blue @ :30 10 x 25 Kick w/fins & chutes underwater @ 1:00
DISTANCE	2 x 400 Paddle w/Pull Buoy @ 4:45/5:00 3 x 200 IM :30 sec 4 x 50 Free @ :40 2 x 300 (150 Free/150 Non-Free) @ 4 x 100 Descend @ 1:30 4 x 50 Free @ :40 4 x 25's Max start + breakout
MID-DISTANCE	3 x 500 max for time, from dive

WEEK 17	Tue Dec 19 2023
WARMUP	2 x 300 #1 Free #2 RIMO (drill fly) 6 x 50 non-free @ :15 rest 5 x 100 Paddle w/Pull Buoy @ 1:30 6 x 50 Pull @ 1:00 2 x 100 Paddle w/Pull Buoy @ 2:30/2:40 4 x 100 Pull @ 1:30 4 x 75 Stroke (long underwater on each wall) @ 1:20 4 x 50 25 build to top speed, 25 easy @ 1:00
MAIN SET	2 x 500 Red (2:00) 2 x 300 Red (2:00) 2 x 100 Red (2:00) 1 x 400 cool down

WEEK 17	Wed Dec 20 2023
WARMUP	1 x 600 (200 Free/200 BK/200 BR) 1 x 400 (200 Kick/200 Choice) 1 x 400 Paddle w/Pull Buoy DPS 4 x 100 IM (drill fly) @ 2:00/2:10 4 x 50 Back @ 1:00 6 x 50 (25 Breast Kick on Back) @ 1:10 4 x 75 (Free/NonFree/Free) @ 1:10 4 x 25 Breast @ :40
SPRINT	1 x 400 (200 White/200 Pink) 2 x 100 IM @ 2:00 10 x 50 @ 1:00 Odds 50 Free Evens 50 NonFree 2 x 200's MAX @ 2:30 2 x 100's MAX @ 1:30 4 x 50's MAX @ :50 4 x 25's MAX @ :30
DISTANCE	8 x 100 IM pink @ 1:50 1 x Broken 1650 1 x 500 Build @ :10 rest 1 x 500 D 100s 1-5 @ :15 rest 1 x 500 Red @ :20 rest 1 x 100 Blue @ :10 rest 1 x 50 MAX 1 x 800 White @ :20 rest 4 x 50 Kick @ 1:00
MID-DISTANCE	2 x 200 Broken @ :50 6 x 50 Red @ 1:00 1 x 500 Free 2 x 200 @ :20 rest #1 Choice #2 Non-Free

WEEK 17	Thu Dec 21 2023
WARMUP	6 x 50 drill/swim @ 1:00 1 x 600 Paddle/Pull Bp 5 by 100's work on great turns 6 x 50 (25 fist/25 pink) @ 1:00 Concentrate on high elbow catch 6 x 50 Free Underwater Recovery Drill @ 1:00 1 x 400 Kick w/fins 5 x 50 Kick w/fins dolphin on back @ :50 6 x 25 underwater MAX kick w/fins @ :25
MAIN SET	8 x 25 IM @ :40 4 x (100 IMO + 50 white) @ 15 rest 3 x 300 @ :20 rest 5 x 100 IMO @ 1:50 #1-3: Descend #4-6 :Descend to Max 5 x 100 JMI @ 1:10

WEEK 17	Fri Dec 22 2023
WARMUP	400 RIMO 6 x 100 Non-Free (50 Kick / 50 Swim) @ :10 rest 12 x 50 (4 x Fly/Free, Back/Free, Breast/Free) @ :10 rest 16 x 50 @ :50 #1-4 sprint turns in & out of flags #5-8 BK 15 yds underwater kick + fast breakout #9-12 free with fast kick #13-16 Fly 25 kick/25 fast
SPRINT	8 x 50 (25 Drill / 25 build to max finish) @ :50 2 x 50 MAX 6 x 25 work on breakout 4 x 50 D 1-4 @ 1:00 8 x 75 (free/kick/non-free) @ 1:20 6 x 150 (BK/free/choice) @ :10 rest
DISTANCE	8 x 50 (25 Drill / 25 build to max finish) @ :50 1 x Broken 200 @ 50 2 x Broken 100 @ 50 & 75 5 x 100 Kick @ 1:50 2 x 100 Pull @ 1:20

MID-DISTANCE	1 x 800
	(200 Pull / 200 Swim / 200 Pull / 200 IM)
	(1:00)
	4 x 200 @ 2:20/2:30
	Pink-Red-Blue-MAX
	10 x 100
	odds: Hold 500 goal pace @ 1:30
	evens: White @ 1:35/1:40
	
	2 x {
	  8 x 50 @ :45
	(:30)
	  4 x 25 underwater @ :40
	}

WEEK 17	Sat Dec 23 2023
WARMUP	500 Free 200 Back 3 x200 #1 Free #2 (Back/Breast by 50's) #3 (100 Choice/100 IM) 4 x 50 choice @ 1:10 2 x 200 Scull #1 Front, #2 Back 4 x 50 Fist Drill @ 1:00 4 x 75 (fist drill/swim/build) @ 1:10

MAIN SET	2 x {
	   1 x 25 MAX from Dive @ :30
	   1 x 100 JMI @ 1:15/1:25
	   1 x 50 kick ½ way underwater on every wall @ :40/:45
	   1 x 25 MAX underwater kick from Dive @ :40
	   1 x 100 MAX for time
	}

DECEMBER — ELITE SWIM WORKOUT '24 — WEEK 18

Monday	Tuesday	Wednesday	Thursday	Friday	Saturday

1 x 400 Free
1 x 300 Non-Free
1 x 200 Kick
1 x 100 IM
 	
2 x {
1 x 300 Kick :30 sec rest
4 x 50 Kick Descend to MAX @ 1:00
6 x 100 Paddle w/Pull Buoy @ 1:20/1:30
6 x 75 Descend @ 1:10
odds: fly-back-breast
evens: back-breast-free
 	
SPRINT
8 x 25 Kick w/chutes @ :45
8 x 25 Swim MAX w/fins @ :40
 	
4 x 200(
#1 8 x 25 @ :25 max of 2 breaths
#2 2 x 100 @ 1:25 (1 Red, 1 Blue)
#3 4 x 50 Kick (1 Red/ 1 White) @ :55
#4 200 Negative Split
}
8 x 50 w/chutes @ 1:20
#1-4 D1-4 , #4-8 Kick D1-4 to Max
 	
DISTANCE
4 x 200
odds: Free @ 2:30/2:40
evens: IM @ 2:30/2:40
 	
8 x (100 IM + 25 easy) @ 2:00/2:15 (2:00)
2 x (50 + 25 easy) @ 1:20/1:30
odds: Fly-Back-Breast Descend
evens: IMO Red
8 x 50 Stroke
#1-4 @ :40/:45
#5-8 Red @ :35/:40
MID-DISTANCE
 	
6 x 75
odds: Fast @ 1:10
evens: Easy @ 1:20
5 x 100 Kick w/fins @ 1:10
200 Cooldown
2 x (10 x 50 @ 1:30) ALL MAX
	3 x 600
	#1 200 RIMO/200 Swim/200 Drill
	#2 300 (50 drill/50 swim best Stroke/300 kick
	)
	#3 Swim Choice
	
	2 x 100 Paddle w/Pull Buoy @ 2:30/2:40
	4 x 100 Pull @ 1:30
	4 x 75 Stroke (long underwater on each wall) @ 1:20
	4 x 50 25 build to top speed, 25 easy @ 1:00
	
	4 x 75 Build each @ 1:20
	4 x 25 MAX Breakout @ :40
	6 x 50 w/fins Fast kick dolphin @ 1:10
	6 x 25 w/fins underwater kick @ :30 (1:00)
	6 x 25 w/chutes JMI @ :50
	6 x 25 w/chutes Build @ :40
	4 x 25 w/chutes MAX @ :40
	
	4 x 100 w/fins dolphin on back @ 1:30
	
	400 Free@ 4:50/5:10
	4 x 50 red @ :50
	300 Bp 7 by 50's @ 3:40/3:50 (2:00)
	4 x 100 Choice@ 1:30/1:40
	4 x 50 Blue @ :40
	1 x 200 BP: 7
		1 x 200 Kick no board
		1 x 200 Kick w/Board
		1 x 200 Kick w/ fins
		1 x Kick on Back
		
		8 x 50 IMO @ :50
		6 x 150 Fins/ 1:30
		1 x 600 Kick @ 11:00
		6 x 50 Kick D1-6 @ 1:00
		1 x 100 MAX Kick
		
		SPRINT
		6 x 100 (white-pink-red-blue) @ 1:15
		4 x 25 red @ 1:00 rest
		2 x 100 Broken @ the 50 and the 75 @ 4:00 rest
		2 x 50 MAX from a dive @ 2:30 rest
		2 x 25 MAX
		
		DISTANCE
		1 x 400 Free
		4 x 100 IMO (optional drill fly) @ :10 rest
		8 x 50 (Fly/Free, Back/Free, Breast/Free, Free/Free) @ :20
		6 x 150 (drill/kick/swim) @ 2:10
		6 x 50 fist drill #1 Stroke @ 1:00
		4 x 25 Build
		
		1 x 400 IM @ 5:40/6:10/6:30
		4 x 50 Kick no board IMO @ :50 (2:00)
		4 x 200 IM @ 3:15/3:30/3:40
		8 x 50 Kick no board #1 Stroke @ :50
		8 x 50 Kick Pink @ :55
		4 x 50 IMO @ :50
		4 x 100 Kick w/ chutes @ :30 sec rest
		
		MID-DISTANCE
		2 x 800 @ 10:00/10:30
		#1 -Build each 100 to Pink
		#2 -Ascend each 100 starting at Pink
		4 x 200 IM @ 2:40/2:50
		#1-2 -(1/2 way underwater on each wall)
		#3-4 -Swim
		
		2 x 600 @ 7:30/8:00
		#1 each 100 - (White)
		#2 each 100 - (50 Pink + 50 Kick no board)
			3 x 200 - #1 Free #2 Non-Free #3 Choice
			4 x 100 IM White
			
			6 x 100 Paddle w/Pull Buoy @ 1:20/1:30
			
			6 x 75 Descend @ 1:10
			odds: fly-back-breast
			evens: back-breast-free
			
			2 x 100 (50FR/50 fly) @ 1:25
			1 x 200 IM @ 2:45
			1 x 300 Fly @ 4:20 Build each 100 to great turn + great walls
			1 x 200 Free White @ 2:30
			1 x 300 (100back/100BR/100FR) @ 4:30
			1 x 200 Fly @ 2:40
			1 x 300 Free @ 3:50
			1 x 400 IM @ 5:25
			3 x 100 Fly @ 1:35
			1 x 200 Free @ 2:45
				1 x 500 Free
				1 x 400 (200 BK/200 BR)
				1 x 300 Scull
				
				3 x {
				1 x 300 Paddle w/Pull Buoy @ 4:00
				3 x 100 Pull @ 1:30
				
				8 x 25 w/fins underwater kick @ :30
				4 x 50 w/fins underwater kick @ 1:00 (Max of 1 breath allowed per 50)
				
				SPRINT
				8 x 100 w/fins Fast kick @ 1:30
				odds: Flutter
				evens: Dolphin
				4 x 50 D 1-4 @ 1:00
				8 x 25 MAX From Dive
				
				DISTANCE
				6 x 125 w/fins (25 kick/50 swim/25 kick/25 dolphin on back) @ 1:50
				2 x 300 White @ 4:00
				4 x 50 D 1-4 @ 1:00
				2 x 200 Pink-Red @ 2:40
				4 x 50 D 1-4 @ 1:00
				2 x 100 White @ 1:35
				4 x 50 Max Breakout @ 1:35
				6 x 50 Kick D1-4 , Hold time on 5-6
				
				MID-DISTANCE
				5 x 200 Neg Split @ 3:00
				5 x {
				200 @ 2:45/2:50 +
				3 x 100 @ 1:30)
				}
				3 x 50 Kick MAX @ 1:45
					200 SKIMPS
					8 x 50 IMO @ :50
					300 White
					
					1 x 300 (150 Kick no board/ 150 Swim) @ 5:30
					1 x 500 white
					2 x 300 Pull @ 3:45/4:00
					10 x 50 @ 1:00
					Odds 50 Free
					Evens 50 Non Free
					
					3 x 100 Kick @ 1:50
					#1 (50 Kick/50 Dolphin Kick)
					#2 (50 Breast Kick/50 Flutter no board)
					#3 Build each 50 to Pink
					4 x 25 Build @ :40
					2 x (10 x 50 KICK @ 1:30) ALL OUT MAX
					1 x 300 Free @ 4:30
					5 x 50 drill Choice @ 1:00
					4 x 100 choice @ 1:40

WEEK 18	Mon Dec 25 2023 - BONUS CHRISTMAS WORKOUT

WARMUP	1 x 400 Free
	1 x 300 Non-Free
	1 x 200 Kick
	1 x 100 IM
	
	2 x {
	1 x 300 Kick :30 sec rest
	4 x 50 Kick Descend to MAX @ 1:00
	}
	6 x 100 Paddle w/Pull Buoy @ 1:20/1:30
	6 x 75 Descend @ 1:10
	odds: fly-back-breast
	evens: back-breast-free

SPRINT	8 x 25 Kick w/chutes @ :45
	8 x 25 Swim MAX w/fins @ :40
	
	4 x 200{
	   #1 8 x 25 @ :25 max of 2 breaths
	   #2 2 x 100 @ 1:25 (1 Red, 1 Blue)
	   #3 4 x 50 Kick (1 Red/1 White) @ :55
	   #4 200 Negative Split
	}
	8 x 50 w/chutes @ 1:20
	#1-4 D1-4 , #4-8 Kick D1-4 to Max

DISTANCE	4 x 200 odds: Free @ 2:30/2:40 evens: IM @ 2:30/2:40 8 x (100 IM + 25 easy) @ 2:00/2:15 (2:00) 8 x (50 + 25 easy) @ 1:20/1:30 odds: Fly-Back-Breast Descend evens: IMO Red 8 x 50 Stroke #1-4 @ :40/:45 #5-8 Red @ :35/:40
MID-DISTANCE	6 x 75 odds: Fast @ 1:10 evens: Easy @ 1:20 5 x 100 Kick w/fins @ 1:10 200 Cooldown 2 x (10 x 50 @ 1:30) ALL MAX

WEEK 18	Tue Dec 26 2023
WARMUP	3 x 600 #1 200 RIMO/200 Swim/200 Drill #2 300 (50 drill/50 swim best Stroke/300 kick) #3 Swim Choice 2 x 100 Paddle w/Pull Buoy @ 2:30/2:40 4 x 100 Pull @ 1:30 4 x 75 - Stroke (long underwater on each wall) @ 1:20 4 x 50 - 25 build to top speed, 25 easy @ 1:00
MAIN SET	4 x 75 Build each @ 1:20 4 x 25 MAX Breakout @ :40 6 x 50 w/fins Fast kick dolphin @ 1:10 6 x 25 w/fins underwater kick @ :30 (1:00) 6 x 25 w/chutes JMI @ :50 6 x 25 w/chutes Build @ :40 4 x 25 w/chutes MAX @ :40 4 x 100 w/fins dolphin on back @ 1:30 400 Free@ 4:50/5:10 4 x 50 red @ :50 300 Bp 7 by 50's @ 3:40/3:50 (2:00) 4 x 100 Choice@ 1:30/1:40 4 x 50 Blue @ :40 1 x 200 BP: 7

WEEK 18	Wed Dec 27 2023
WARMUP	1 x 200 Kick no board 1 x 200 Kick w/Board 1 x 200 Kick w/ fins 1 x Kick on Back 8 x 50 IMO @ :50 6 x 150 Fins/ @ 1:30 1 x 600 Kick @ 11:00 6 x 50 Kick D1-6 @ 1:00 1 x 100 MAX Kick
SPRINT	6 x 100 (white-pink-red-blue) @ 1:15 4 x 25 red @ 1:00 rest 2 x 100 Broken @ the 50 and the 75 @ 4:00 rest 2 x 50 MAX from a dive @ 2:30 rest 2 x 25 MAX
DISTANCE	1 x 400 Free 4 x 100 IMO (optional drill fly) @ :10 rest 8 x 50 (Fly/Free, Back/Free, Breast/Free, Free/Free) @ :20 6 x 150 (drill/kick/swim) @ 2:10 6 x 50 fist drill #1 Stroke @ 1:00 4 x 25 Build 1 x 400 IM @ 5:40/6:10/6:30 4 x 50 Kick no board IMO @ :50 (2:00) 4 x 200 IM @ 3:15/3:30/3:40 8 x 50 Kick no board #1 Stroke @ :50 8 x 50 Kick Pink @ :55 4 x 50 IMO @ :50 4 x 100 Kick w/ chutes @ :30 sec rest
MID-DISTANCE	2 x 800 @ 10:00/10:30 #1 -Build each 100 to Pink #2 -Ascend each 100 starting at Pink 4 x 200 IM @ 2:40/2:50 #1-2 -(1/2 way underwater on each wall) #3-4 -Swim 2 x 600 @ 7:30/8:00 #1 each 100 - (White) #2 each 100 - (50 Pink + 50 Kick no board)

WEEK 18	Thu Dec 28 2023
WARMUP	3 x 200 - #1 Free #2 Non-Free #3 Choice 4 x 100 IM White 6 x 100 Paddle w/Pull Buoy @ 1:20/1:30 6 x 75 Descend @ 1:10 odds: fly-back-breast evens: back-breast-free
MAIN SET	2 x 100 (50FR/50 fly) @ 1:25 1 x 200 IM @ 2:45 1 x 300 Fly @ 4:20 Build each 100 to great turn + great walls 1 x 200 Free White @ 2:30 1 x 300 (100back/100BR/100FR) @ 4:30 1 x 200 Fly @ 2:40 1 x 300 Free @ 3:50 1 x 400 IM @ 5:25 3 x 100 Fly @ 1:35 1 x 200 Free @ 2:45

WEEK 18	Fri Dec 29 2023

WARMUP	1 x 500 Free
	1 x 400 (200 BK / 200 BR)
	1 x 300 Scull
	3 x {
	   1 x 300 Paddle w/ Pull Buoy @ 4:00
	   3 x 100 Pull @ 1:30
	}
	8 x 25 w/ fins underwater kick @ :30
	4 x 50 w/ fins underwater kick @ 1:00
	(Max of 1 breath allowed per 50)

SPRINT	8 x 100 w/ fins Fast kick @ 1:30 odds: Flutter evens: Dolphin 4 x 50 D 1-4 @ 1:00 8 x 25 MAX From Dive
DISTANCE	6 x 125 w/ fins (25 kick/50 swim/25 kick/25 dolphin on back) @ 1:50 2 x 300 White @ 4:00 4 x 50 D 1-4 @ 1:00 2 x 200 Pink-Red @ 2:40 4 x 50 D 1-4 @ 1:00 2 x 100 White @ 1:35 4 x 50 Max Breakout @ 1:35 6 x 50 Kick D1-4 , Hold time on 5-6

MID-DISTANCE	5 x 200 Neg Split @ 3:00
	5 x {
	   200 @ 2:45/2:50 +
	   3 x 100 @ 1:30)
	}
	3 x 50 Kick MAX @ 1:45

WEEK 18	Sat Dec 30 2023
WARMUP	200 SKIMPS 8 x 50 IMO @ :50 300 White 1 x 300 (150 Kick no board / 150 Swim) @ 5:30 1 x 500 white 2 x 300 Pull @ 3:45/4:00 10 x 50 @ 1:00 Odds 50 Free Evens 50 Non Free 3 x 100 Kick @ 1:50 #1 (50 Kick / 50 Dolphin Kick) #2 (50 Breast Kick / 50 Flutter no board) #3 Build each 50 to Pink
MAIN SET	4 x 25 Build @ :40 2 x (10 x 50 KICK @ 1:30) ALL OUT MAX 1 x 300 Free @ 4:30 5 x 50 drill Choice @ 1:00 4 x 100 choice @ 1:40

Monday	Tuesday	Wednesday	Thursday	Friday	Saturday

2 x 200
#1 Kick Choice
#2 Kick no Board
200 IM
 	
6 x 75 @ 1:20
50 drill/25 swim
 	
8 x 50 (25 Drill/ 25 build to max finish) @ :50
5 x 100 Stroke @ 1:10/1:20/1:30/1:40
 	
SPRINT
 	
8 x 50 (25 Drill/ 25 build to max finish) @ :50
 	
1 x Broken 200 @ 50
2 x 50 MAX
Cool Down
 	
DISTANCE
 	
4 x 200 Max for time, from dive
MID-DISTANCE
 	
10 x (50 + 50 easy)
Hold 500 Goal Pace - 5 (2:00)
3 x 300 neg split + 100 easy
200 red + 100 easy
100 red + 50 easy
50 max + 50 easy
 	
1 x 800 Fin Swim (1:00)
5 x 100 w/fins @ 1:20/1:35
add up to best time 500
	3 x 300
	#1 Free
	#2 Back
	#2 (150 Kick/150 Swim choice)
	
	4 x 50 choice @ 1:10
	
	3 x 300 (100 Moderate/100 Drill/100 Build to Pink) @ 3:50/4:00/4:10
	4 x 100 Negative Split (50 White/50 Red) @ 1:10/1:20
	4 x 50 @ :40
	
	3 x 500 @ 7:30/7:50
	Bp 3-5-7-5-3 by 100s
	4 x 400 Paddle/Pull D 1-4 @ 5:20
	6 x 150 (fly/back/BR) w/ fins @ 2:10
	
	6 x 150 @ 2:00
	D 1-3, 4-6 to MAX
		4 x 200
		IM-NonFree-Free-Kick
		1 x 400
		
		SPRINT
		
		4 x {
		1 x 200 Blue (:30)
		1 x 100 Red (:30)
		1 x 50 Red (1:00)
		}
		
		1 x 300 cool down
		
		DISTANCE
		
		1 x 400 (100 Free/100 Back)
		2 x 200 Stroke@ 2:30/2:40
		Pink - Red
		4 x 50 (12.5 underwater MAX kick + MAX breakout/12.5 easy swim) @ 1:00
		
		2 x {
		1 x 25 MAX from Dive @ :30
		1 x 75 JMI @ 1:15
		1 x 50 kick ½ way underwater on every wall @ :40/:45
		1 x 25 MAX underwater kick from Dive @ :40
		1 x 100 MAX for time
		}
		MID-DISTANCE
		
		1 x 400 Free
		4 x 100 IMO (optional drill fly) @ :10 rest
		8 x 50 (Fly/Free, Back/Free, Breast/Free, Free/Free) @ :20
		
		6 x 150 (drill/kick/swim) @ 2:10
		6 x 50 fist drill #1 Stroke @ 1:00
		4 x 25 Build
		
		1 x 400 IM @ 5:40/6:10/6:30
		4 x 50 Kick no board IMO @ :50 (2:00)
		4 x 200 IM @ 3:15/3:30/3:40
		8 x 50 Kick no board #1 Stroke @ :50
		
		8 x 50 Kick Pink @ :55
		4 x 50 IMO @ :50
		4 x 100 Kick w/ chutes @ :30 sec rest
			1 x 500 Free
			1 x 300 Scull
			
			8 x 50 (25 Drill/ 25 build to max finish) @ :50
			5 x 100 Stroke @ 1:10/1:20/1:30/1:40
			
			5 x 200 Best Average @ 3:30/4:00
			3 x 100 @ 1:30 white
			3 x 400 @ 5:20
			Clear-White-Pink
			4 x 50 Kick MAX @ 1:00 (1:00)
			4 x 300 @ 3:30/3:40
			(1)Pink - (2) Red - (1)Blue
			4 x 50 Kick MAX
				400 IM
				6 x 100 Kick w/Board
				4 x 100 IM Order @ :15 rest
				
				4 x 75 (25 fist drill/25 swim/25 build) @ 1:20
				8 x 50 (25 kick no board/25 swim) @ 1:00
				
				SPRINT
				
				3 x 200 1 white, 1 pink, 1 red @ 2:40
				8 x 100 4 white, 2 pink, 2 red @ 1:20
				4 x 50 Goal 200 Pace @ 1:00
				8 x 100 (50 Blue/50 choice) @ 2:00
				
				Cooldown – 4 x 100 choice @ 1:40
				DISTANCE
				
				6 x 100 Stroke@ 1:30
				Odds: Work Turns
				Evens: Work Finish
				
				1 x 400 (200 White/200 Pink) + 100 easy
				4 x (200 + 100 easy)
				D 1-4
				8 x (100 + 50 easy)
				D 1-4, Hold 5-8
				8 x (50 MAX + 50 easy)
				
				MID-DISTANCE
				
				5 x 125 @ 1:50/2:00
				#1-3 100 Pink + 25 Red w/2 Breaths
				#4-6 100 Red + 25 MAX w/2 Breaths
				
				6 x 150 @ 3:30 (50 Kick Blue + 100 Swim)
				12 x 50 @ :50
					2 x 200 #1 Free, #2 Non-Free
					4 x 100 IM :20 sec-6 x 50 @ 1:00 2 fist drill, 1 build3 x 100 Kick @ 1:50
					Sprint
					
					5 x 200 :20
					#1 Kick
					#2 Paddle w/Pull Buoy White
					#3 Paddle w/Pull Buoy Pink
					#4 Paddle w/Pull Buoy Red
					#5 Kick
					
					5 x 100 @ 1:40
					odds: Build each 25 to MAX flip
					evens: Build each 25 to MAX finish

WEEK 19	Mon Jan 01 2024
WARMUP	2 x 200 #1 Kick Choice #2 Kick no Board 200 IM 6 x 75 @ 1:20 50 drill/25 swim 8 x 50 (25 Drill / 25 build to max finish) @ :50 5 x 100 Stroke @ 1:10/1:20/1:30/1:40
SPRINT	8 x 50 (25 Drill / 25 build to max finish) @ :50 1 x Broken 200 @ 50 2 x 50 MAX Cool Down
DISTANCE	4 x 200 Max for time, from dive
MID-DISTANCE	10 x (50 + 50 easy) Hold 500 Goal Pace - .5 (2:00) 3 x 300 neg split + 100 easy 200 red + 100 easy 100 red + 50 easy 50 max + 50 easy 1 x 800 Fin Swim (1:00) 5 x 100 w/fins @ 1:20/1:35 add up to best time 500

WEEK 19	Tue Jan 02 2024
WARMUP	3 x 300 #1 Free #2 Back #2 (150 Kick / 150 Swim choice) 4 x 50 choice @ 1:10 3 x 300 (100 Moderate / 100 Drill / 100 Build to Pink) @ 3:50 / 4:00 / 4:10 4 x 100 Negative Split (50 White / 50 Red) @ 1:10 / 1:20 4 x 50 @ :40 3 x 500 @ 7:30 / 7:50 Bp 3-5-7-5-3 by 100s 4 x 400 Paddle / Pull D 1-4 @ 5:20
MAIN SET	6 x 150 (fly / back / BR) w/ fins @ 2:10 6 x 150 @ 2:00 D 1-3, 4-6 to MAX

WEEK 19	Wed Jan 03 2024
WARMUP	4 x 200 IM-NonFree-Free-Kick 1 x 400

SPRINT	4 x {
	   1 x 200 Blue
	   (:30)
	   1 x 100 Red
	   (:30)
	   1 x 50 Red
	   (1:00)
	     }
	1 x 300 cool down

DISTANCE	1 x 400 (100 Free/100 Back)
	2 x 200 Stroke@ 2:30/2:40
	Pink – Red
	4 x 50 (12.5 underwater MAX kick + MAX breakout/12.5 easy swim) @ 1:00
	
	2 x {
	   1 x 25 MAX from Dive @ :30
	   1 x 75 JMI @ 1:15
	   1 x 50 kick ½ way underwater on every wall @ :40/:45
	   1 x 25 MAX underwater kick from Dive @ :40
	   1 x 100 MAX for time
	}
	6 x 100 @ 1:40

MID-DISTANCE	1 x 400 Free 4 x 100 IMO (optional drill fly) @ :10 rest 8 x 50 (Fly/Free, Back/Free, Breast/Free, Free/Free) @ :20 6 x 150 (drill/kick/swim) @ 2:10 6 x 50 fist drill #1 Stroke @ 1:00 4 x 25 Build 1 x 400 IM @ 5:40/6:10/6:30 4 x 50 Kick no board IMO @ :50 (2:00) 4 x 200 IM @ 3:15/3:30/3:40 8 x 50 Kick no board #1 Stroke @ :50 8 x 50 Kick Pink @ :55 4 x 50 IMO @ :50 4 x 100 Kick w/ chutes @ :30 sec rest

WEEK 19	Thu Jan 04 2024
WARMUP	1 x 500 Free 1 x 300 Scull 8 x 50 (25 Drill/ 25 build to max finish) @ :50 5 x 100 Stroke @ 1:10/1:20/1:30/1:40 5 x 200 Best Average @ 3:30/4:00 3 x 100 @ 1:30 white 3 x 400 @ 5:20 Clear-White-Pink
MAIN SET	4 x 50 Kick MAX @ 1:00 (1:00) 4 x 300 @ 3:30/3:40 (1)Pink - (2) Red – (1)Blue 4 x 50 Kick MAX

WEEK 19	Fri Jan 05 2024
WARMUP	400 IM 6 x 100 Kick w/Board 4 x 100 IM Order @ :15 rest 4 x 75 (25 fist drill/25 swim/25 build) @ 1:20 8 x 50 (25 kick no board/25 swim) @ 1:00
SPRINT	3 x 200 1 white, 1 pink, 1 red @ 2:40 8 x 100 4 white, 2 pink, 2 red @ 1:20 4 x 50 Goal 200 Pace @ 1:00 8 x 100 (50 Blue/50 choice) @ 2:00 Cooldown – 4 x 100 choice @ 1:40
DISTANCE	6 x 100 Stroke@ 1:30 Odds: Work Turns Evens: Work Finish 1 x 400 (200 White/200 Pink) + 100 easy 4 x (200 + 100 easy) D 1-4 8 x (100 + 50 easy) D 1-4 , Hold 5-8 8 x (50 MAX + 50 easy)
MID-DISTANCE	5 x 125 @ 1:50/2:00 #1-3 100 Pink + 25 Red w/2 Breaths #4-6 100 Red + 25 MAX w/2 Breaths 6 x 150 @ 3:30 (50 Kick Blue + 100 Swim) 12 x 50 @ :50

WEEK 19	Sat Jan 06 2024
WARMUP	2 x 200 #1 Free, #2 Non-Free 4 x 100 IM :20 sec6 x 50 @ 1:00 2 fist drill, 1 build3 x 100 Kick @ 1:50
MAIN SET	5 x 200 :20 #1 Kick #2 Paddle w/Pull Buoy White #3 Paddle w/Pull Buoy Pink #4 Paddle w/Pull Buoy Red #5 Kick 5 x 100 @ 1:40 odds: Build each 25 to MAX flip evens: Build each 25 to MAX finish

Monday	Tuesday	Wednesday	Thursday	Friday	Saturday

1 x 400 (200 Free/200 Back)
1 x 300 (150 kick non-free/150 kick breast)
1 x 200 (100 BK/100 Choice)
1 x 100 IM
2 x {
3 x 50 fist drill @ 1:00
8 x 25 #1 Stroke drill @ :45
fly: press/pop, back catchup, Breast: pull w/ little paddles, Free: single arm
4 x 25 build @ :30
}
4 x 100 (50 #1 Stroke/50 Free) @ 1:30
Stroke – easy free
 	
SPRINT
4 x 50s RED
2 x 50 MAX from Dive
1 x 400 Fin Swim
3 x 25 Chutes underwater kick w/fins
 	
3 x 300 @ 4:00
3 x 100 D1-3 @ 1:20
 	
DISTANCE
5 x 100 @ 1:20 (no breath in or out of walls) @ 1:30
8 x 50 (25 Drill/ 25 build to max finish) @ :50
 	
4 x (300 + 100 easy)
odds: 100 Swim/100 Kick RED/100 Swim
evens: Descend each 100 (1:30)
4 x (200 + 50 easy)
#1 Pink, #2 Drop 5 secs, #3 MAX Kick, #4 Drop 3 sec from #2
8 x (50 + 50 easy) Descend 1-4 , hold time on 5-8
 	
MID-DISTANCE
3 x 300 @ 3:45/3:55
White-Pink-Red
4 x 100 JMI @ 1:10/1:20 (1:00)
4 x 100 @ 1:20/1:30 Red-Blue-(2) MAX (2:00)
6 x 50 @ 1:00
	200 SKIMPS
	1 x 500 Kick
	
	5 x 50 Dolphin on Back @ :50
	
	12 x 75 Continuous IM @ 1:10
	4 x 25 IMO Descend @ :30
	
	3 x 200 Paddle/Pull
	6 x 50 max of 2 breaths @ 1:00
	8 x 200 IMO @ 2:40
	
	15 x 100
	odds: Free @ 1:20
	evens: IM @ 1:30
		2 x 200 #1 Free, #2 Non-Free
		4 x 100 IM :20 sec6 x 50 @ 1:00 2 fist drill, 1 build3 x 100 Kick @ 1:50
		Sprint
		
		8 x 50 @ :50
		odds: build into first wall, great turn
		evens: build into finish, great finish
		2 x {
		4 x 25 (drill,build,drill,MAX) @ :40
		}
		SPRINT
		10 x 50 kick @ 1:00
		
		1 x 100 Broken @ 25's
		1 x 50s MAX
		6 x 25
		#1-3 MAX breakout
		#4-6 build
		
		6 x 100 (50 free/50 kick@ 1:20
		4 x 150 choice
		
		DISTANCE
		3 x {
		1 x (300 + 100 easy)
		4 x (50 + 50 MAX)
		}
		4 x 50 MAX Kick no board @1:00
		
		MID-DISTANCE
		2 x 800 (400 White/400 Red) @ :30 sec rest (1:00)
		4 x (200 + 50 easy)
		odds: Pink
		evens: Max Turns (1:00)
		8 x (100 + 50 easy)
		D1-4 , Hold #4 time on 5-8
			4 x 200
			IM-NonFree-Free-Kick
			
			10 x 25 Build each 25 to fast flip @ 1:10
			8 x 25 (12.5 underwater kick sprint/12.5 breakout MAX, easy) @ :30
			
			1 x 200 Choice
			6 x 50 Paddle @ :50
			
			1 x 300 Build @ 3:15/3:30
			4 x 50 @ :35/:40
			
			2 x 200 Choice @ 3:00
				200 SKIMPS
				Pull- (2 x 25 Choice/75 Swim)
				
				2 x {
				3 x 50 fist drill @ 1:00
				8 x 25 #1 Stroke drill @ :45
				fly: press/pop, back: catchup, Breast: pull w/ little paddles, Free: single arm
				4 x 25 build @ :30
				}
				4 x 100 (50 #1 Stroke/50 Free) @ 1:30
				Stroke – easy free
				
				SPRINT
				1 x 25 MAX from Dive @ :30
				1 x 75 JMI @ 1:10/1:15
				1 x 50 kick ½ way underwater on every wall @ :40/:45
				1 x 25 MAX underwater kick from Dive @ :40
				1 x 100 MAX for time
				
				DISTANCE
				3 x 300
				#1 Free
				#2 Kick/Swim by 50's
				#3 Best Stroke/ Worst Stroke by 50's
				
				4 x 100 RIMO @ 1:30
				8 x 50 (Fly/Free, Back/Free, Breast/Free, Free/Free) :50
				2 x (4 x 50 w/fins kick dolphin on back @ :45
				4 x 25 Build Kick w/fins @ :30
				1 x 200 MAX Kick w/fins @ 4:30
				9 x 125
				#1-3 100 Build + 25 Red 2 breaths @ 1:50
				#4-6 50 White + 75 Red @ 1:40
				#7-9 25 MAX no breath + 75 White + 25 1 breath
				
				MID-DISTANCE
				5 x {
				400 @ 4:30/4:45/4:50
				4 x 100 Goal 500 Pace @ 1:10/1:15/1:20
				1:00 rest
				}
					1 x 500 (200 Free/200 Non-Free/100 RIMO)
					8 x 100 @ :10 rest
					odds: #1 Stroke (50 drill/50 swim)
					evens: (50 BK/50 BR)
					
					12 x 75 @
					#1-4 (50 Free/25 BK)
					#5-8 (25 Kick no board/50 Breast)
					#9-12 (Fly/Back/Breast)
					4 x 200 Paddle/Pull
					8 x 50 @ :50
					
					5x 200 @ :10(100 Pink/50 Build /50 White)
					
					10 x 100 JMI
					#1-5 @ 1:10/1:15
					#6-10 @ 1:05/1:10 (2:00)
					8 x 50 @ :35/:40

WEEK 20	Mon Jan 08 2024

WARMUP	1 x 400 (200 Free/200 Back)
	1 x 300 (150 Kick non-free/150 kick breast)
	1 x 200 (100 BK/100 Choice)
	1 x 100 IM
	2 x {
	   3 x 50 fist drill @ 1:00
	   8 x 25 #1 Stroke drill @ :45
	   fly: press/pop, back: catchup, Breast: pull w/ little paddles, Free: single arm
	   4 x 25 build @ :30
	}
	4 x 100 (50 #1 Stroke/50 Free) @ 1:30
	 Stroke – easy free

SPRINT	4 x 50s RED 2 x 50 MAX from Dive 1 x 400 Fin Swim 3 x 25 Chutes underwater kick w/fins 3 x 300 @ 4:00 3 x 100 D1-3 @ 1:20
DISTANCE	5 x 100 @ 1:20 (no breath in or out of walls) @ 1:30 8 x 50 (25 Drill/ 25 build to max finish) @ :50 4 x (300 + 100 easy) odds: 100 Swim/100 Kick RED/100 Swim evens: Descend each 100 (1:30) 4 x (200 + 50 easy) #1 Pink, #2 Drop 5 secs, #3 MAX Kick, #4 Drop 3 sec from #2 (1:00) 8 x (50 + 50 easy) Descend 1-4 , hold time on 5-8
MID-DISTANCE	3 x 300 @ 3:45/3:55 White-Pink-Red 4 x 100 JMI @ 1:10/1:20 (1:00) 4 x 100 @ 1:20/1:30 Red-Blue-(2) MAX (2:00) 6 x 50 @ 1:00

WEEK 20	Tue Jan 09 2024
WARMUP	200 SKIMPS 1 x 500 Kick 5 x 50 Dolphin on Back @ :50 12 x 75 Continuous IM @ 1:10 4 x 25 IMO Descend @ :30
MAIN SET	3 x 200 Paddle / Pull 6 x 50 max of 2 breaths @ 1:00 8 x 200 IMO @ 2:40 15 x 100 odds: Free @ 1:20 evens: IM @ 1:30

WEEK 20	Wed Jan 10 2024

WARMUP	2 x 200 #1 Free, #2 Non-Free
	4 x 100 IM :20 sec6 x 50 @ 1:00 2 fist drill, 1 build3 x 100 Kick @ 1:50 Sprint
	
	8 x 50 @ :50
	odds: build into first wall, great turn
	evens: build into finish, great finish
	
	2 x {
	   4 x 25 (drill,build,drill,MAX) @ :40
	}

SPRINT	10 x 50 kick @ 1:00 1 x 100 Broken @ 25's 1 x 50 MAX 6 x 25 #1-3 MAX breakout #4-6 build 6 x 100 (50 free/50 kick@ 1:20 4 x 150 choice

DISTANCE	3 x {
	   1 x (300 + 100 easy)
	   4 x (50 + 50 MAX)
	}
	4 x 50 MAX Kick no board @ 1:00

MID-DISTANCE	2 x 800 (400 White/400 Red) @ :30 sec rest (1:00) 4 x (200 + 50 easy) odds: Pink evens: Max Turns (1:00) 8 x (100 + 50 easy) D1-4 , Hold #4 time on 5-8

WEEK 20	Thu Jan 11 2024
WARMUP	4 x 200 IM-NonFree-Free-Kick 10 x 25 Build each 25 to fast flip @ 1:10 8 x 25 (12.5 underwater kick sprint/12.5 breakout MAX, easy) @ :30
MAIN SET	1 x 200 Choice 6 x 50 Paddle @ :50 1 x 300 Build @ 3:15/3:30 4 x 50 @ :35/:40 2 x 200 Choice @ 3:00

WEEK 20	Fri Jan 12 2024

WARMUP	200 SKIMPS
	Pull- (2 x 25 Choice/75 Swim)
	2 x {
	   3 x 50 fist drill @ 1:00
	   8 x 25 #1 Stroke drill @ :45
	   fly: press/pop, back: catchup, Breast: pull w/ little paddles, Free: single arm
	   4 x 25 build @ :30
	}
	4 x 100 (50 #1 Stroke/50 Free) @ 1:30
	 Stroke – easy free

SPRINT	1 x 25 MAX from Dive @ :30 1 x 75 JMI @ 1:10/1:15 1 x 50 kick ½ way underwater on every wall @ :40/:45 1 x 25 MAX underwater kick from Dive @ :40 1 x 100 MAX for time
DISTANCE	3 x 300 #1 Free #2 Kick/Swim by 50's #3 Best Stroke/ Worst Stroke by 50's 4 x 100 RIMO @ 1:30 8 x 50 (Fly/Free, Back/Free, Breast/Free, Free/Free) :50 2 x {4 x 50 w/fins kick dolphin on back @ :45 4 x 25 Build Kick w/fins @ :30 1 x 200 MAX Kick w/fins @ 4:30 } 9 x 125 #1-3 100 Build + 25 Red 2 breaths @ 1:50 #4-6 50 White + 75 Red @ 1:40 #7-9 25 MAX no breath + 75 White + 25 1 breath

MID-DISTANCE	5 x {
	   400 @ 4:30/4:45/4:50
	   4 x 100 Goal 500 Pace @ 1:10/1:15/1:20
	   1:00 rest
	}

WEEK 20	Sat Jan 13 2024
WARMUP	1 x 500 (200 Free/200 Non-Free/100 RIMO) 8 x 100 @ :10 rest odds: #1 Stroke (50 drill/50 swim) evens: (50 Bk/50 BR) 12 x 75 @ #1-4 (50 Free/25 BK) #5-8 (25 Kick no board/50 Breast) #9-12 (Fly/Back/Breast) 4 x 200 Paddle/Pull 8 x 50 @ :50
MAIN SET	5x 200 @ :10(100 Pink/50 Build /50 White) 10 x 100 JMI #1-5 @ 1:10/1:15 #6-10 @ 1:05/1:10 (2:00) 8 x 50 @ :35/:40

JANUARY ELITE SWIM WORKOUT '24 WEEK 21

Monday	Tuesday	Wednesday	Thursday	Friday	Saturday

3 x 300
#1 Free
#2 Back
#2 (150 Kick/150 Swim choice)
 	
6 x 100 DPS @ :50
 	
SPRINT
 	
1 x 300 w/fins work long wall
2 x 200 @ 2:30
#1 Build each 25 to Max FLIP
#2 Build each 50 to Pink
 	
2 x {
4 x 100 Neg Split @ 1:30 (White/Pink)
4 x 50 Descend BP-5
4 x 25 work each finish
}
4 x 150 choice
 	
DISTANCE
 	
2 x 300 White- Pink @ 3:50
3 x 100 Descend @ 1:30
8 x 100 Negative Split @ 1:40
4 x 50 D 1-4 @ 1:00
4 x 100 White BP-5 by 50's @ 1:30
10 x 100 Build to great finish @ 1:20
 	
MID-DISTANCE
 	
1 x 500 MAX
3 x 200 MAX
	200 SK:MPS
	Pull: (2 x 25 Choice/75 Swim)
	
	6 x 75 (Kick/drill/swim) @ 1:10
	8 x 25 @ :30
	odds: drill/ evens: stroke
	
	5 x 100 @ 1:40
	odds: Build each 25 to MAX flip
	evens: Build each 25 to MAX finish
	
	1 x 400 @ 4:50/5:10
	4 x 100 @ 1:10/1:20
	Negative Split (White/Red)
	
	1 x 800 @ 9:30/10:15
	4 x 200 @ 2:30/2:40
	
	6 x 50 @ 1:00
	odds: 25 underwater/25 swim
	evens: 25 swim no breath/25 choice
	
	4 x 100 (50 Non-Free/25 back/25 Choice) @ 1:50
		2 x 300 DPS @ 4:00
		5 x 100 (3) White (2) Pink @ 1:30
		
		6 x 50 Fist Drill @ 1:00 6 x 25 Build to great finish @ :30
		
		2 x {
		1 x 300 Kick (150 White w/board/150 Pink no board) @ 5:45
		4 x 50 Descend to MAX @ 1:00
		4 x 25 Dolphin on back @ :30
		}
		
		SPRINT
		
		1 x 400 Free Bp 3,5 by 100
		6 x 100 Non Free @ 1:50
		
		2 x {
		1 x 400 IM @ :20 rest
		4 x 100 Free Descend @ 1:30
		}
		
		2 x {
		2 x 300 (100 Free/100 Non Free/100 IM) @ :15 rest
		4 x 100 (50 Free/50 Non Free) @ 1:40
		}
		
		DISTANCE
		
		10 x 50 @ 4:00
		#1-3 MAX of 3 Breaths
		#4-6 MAX of 2 Breaths
		#7-9 MAX of 1 Breath
		#10 No Breath
		
		4 x (75+ 25 easy)
		Descend
		8 x (50 + 50 easy)
		Round 1 all red
		Round 2 all MAX
		
		MID-DISTANCE
		
		4 x 100 IM @ 1:50 Pink
		
		12 x 50 Fins @ :40
		4 x 50 #1 drill, #2 build, #3 drill, #4 sprint @ :30
		
		3 x {
		200 White @ 2:40
		2 x 75 Pink @ 1:30
		4 x 50 Red @ 1:00
		2 x 25 MAX @ :40
		(2:00 rest)
		}
			1 x 400 Free
			1 x 300 Non-Free
			1 x 200 Kick
			1 x 100 IM
			
			2 x {
			1 x 300 Kick :30 sec rest
			4 x 50 Kick Descend to MAX @ 1:00
			}
			
			4 x 100 IMO (Kick/Drill/Swim/Drill) @ 2:20
			3 x 200 Free
			4 x 25 kick red @ :30
			
			IM
			200 IM (50 Kick/50 Swim) @ 4:00
			
			6 x 25 w/chutes @ 1:10
			D1-6
			(1:00)
			6 x 25 w/chutes Build@ :45
			4 x 25 w/chutes MAX@ :45
			
			6 x 25 w/fins underwater kick @ :30
			4 x 50 IMO @ :45/:50
			4 x 100 Free Bp 5@ 1:30/1:40
			(2:00)
			3 x 100 IM @ 1:20/1:30
			4 x 50 IMO @ :45/:50
			(1:00)
			6 x 50 w/fins Fast kick dolphin @ 1:00
			1 x 400 w/fins dolphin on back
				3 x 200 Free
				1 x 100 Kick Fly
				3 x 100 Freestyle
				
				2 x 100 Paddle w/Pull Buoy @ 2:30/2:40
				4 x 100 Pull @ 1:30
				
				4 x 75 Stroke (long underwater on each wall) @ 1:20
				4 x 50 25 build to top speed, 25 easy @ 1:00
				
				SPRINT
				
				3 x 200 Best Average @ 3:00/3:10
				4 x 50 Avg. Best time@ 1:00
				2 x 50's max for time
				
				DISTANCE
				
				3 x { @ 12:00
				1 x 200 @ 3:00 Dive
				Go 500 Pace
				2 x 100 @ 1:40
				Goal going out 200 pace for 500
				1 x 100 Dive MAX
				
				10 x 50 @ 1:00
				Odds 50 Kick
				Evens 50 Swim
				
				MID-DISTANCE
				
				Mile MAX for time
				2 x 400 Paddle w/Pull Buoy
					4 x 300 Free-Kick-RIMO - (50 Swim/50 Drill)
					
					2 x {
					4 x 50 Fist Drill @ 1:10
					2 x 25 Build to Pink @ :30
					}
					
					IM
					8 x 200 IMO @ :30 rest
					2 x 200 IM @ 2:50
					Pink-Red
					(2:00)
					4 x 200 @ :20 rest
					#1 IM (50 drill/50 swim Pink)
					#2 RIMO (50 Kick Red no board/50 Swim)
					4 x 100 IMO @ 1:30
					Pink-Red-Blue-MAX

WEEK 21	Mon Jan 15 2024
WARMUP	3 x 300 #1 Free #2 Back #2 (150 Kick / 150 Swim choice) 6 x 100 DPS @ :50

SPRINT	1 x 300 w/ fins work long wall
	2 x 200 @ 2:30
	#1 Build each 25 to Max FLIP
	#2 Build each 50 to Pink
	2 x {
	   4 x 100 Neg Split @ 1:30
	   (White / Pink)
	   4 x 50 Descend BP: 5
	   4 x 25 work each finish
	}
	4 x 150 choice

DISTANCE	2 x 300 White- Pink @ 3:50 3 x 100 Descend @ 1:30 8 x 100 Negative Split @ 1:40 4 x 50 D 1-4 @ 1:00 4 x 100 White BP:5 by 50's @ 1:30 10 x 100 Build to great finish @ 1:20
MID-DISTANCE	1 x 500 MAX 3 x 200 MAX

WEEK 21	Tue Jan 16 2024
WARMUP	200 SKIMPS Pull- (2 x 25 Choice/75 Swim) 6 x 75 (Kick/drill/swim) @ 1:10 8 x 25 @ :30 odds: drill/ evens: stroke 5 x 100 @ 1:40 odds: Build each 25 to MAX flip evens: Build each 25 to MAX finish 1 x 400 @ 4:50/5:10 4 x 100 @ 1:10/1:20 Negative Split (White/Red)
MAIN SET	1 x 800 @ 9:30/10:15 4 x 200 @ 2:30/2:40 6 x 50 @ 1:00 odds: 25 underwater/25 swim evens: 25 swim no breath/25 choice 4 x 100 (50 Non-Free/25 back/25 Choice) @ 1:50

WEEK 21	Wed Jan 17 2024

WARMUP	2 x 300 DPS @ 4:00
	5 x 100 (3) White (2) Pink @ 1:30
	
	6 x 50 Fist Drill @ 1:006 x 25 Build to great finish @ :30
	
	2 x {
	   1 x 300 Kick (150 White w/board/150 Pink no board) @ 5:45
	   4 x 50 Descend to MAX @ 1:00
	   4 x 25 Dolphin on back @ :30
	}

SPRINT	1 x 400 Free Bp 3,5 by 100
	6 x 100 Non Free @ 1:50
	
	2 x {
	   1 x 400 IM @ :20 rest
	   4 x 100 Free Descend @ 1:30
	}
	2 x {
	   2 x 300 (100 Free/100 Non Free/100 IM) @ :15 rest
	   4 x 100 (50 Free/50 Non Free) @ 1:40
	}

DISTANCE	10 x 50 @ 4:00 #1-3 MAX of 3 Breaths #4-6 MAX of 2 Breaths #7-9 MAX of 1 Breath #10 No Breath 4 x (75+ 25 easy) Descend 8 x (50 + 50 easy) Round 1 all red Round 2 all MAX

MID-DISTANCE	4 x 100 IM @ 1:50 Pink
	
	12 x 50 Fins @ :40
	4 x 50 #1 drill, #2 build, #3 drill, #4 sprint @ :30
	
	3 x {
	   200 White @ 2:40
	   2 x 75 Pink @ 1:30
	   4 x 50 Red @ 1:00
	   2 x 25 MAX @ :40
	   (2:00 rest)
	}

WEEK 21	Thu Jan 18 2024

WARMUP	1 x 400 Free
	1 x 300 Non-Free
	1 x 200 Kick
	1 x 100 IM
	
	2 x {
	1 x 300 Kick :30 sec rest
	4 x 50 Kick Descend to MAX @ 1:00
	}
	
	4 x 100 IMO (Kick/Drill/Swim/Drill) @ 2:20
	3 x 200 Free
	4 x 25 kick red @ :30

MAIN SET	200 IM (50 Kick/50 Swim) @ 4:00 6 x 25 w/chutes @ 1:10 D1-6 (1:00) 6 x 25 w/chutes Build@ :45 4 x 25 w/chutes MAX@ :45 6 x 25 w/fins underwater kick @ :30 4 x 50 IMO @ :45/:50 4 x 100 Free Bp 5@ 1:30/1:40 (2:00) 3 x 100 IM @ 1:20/1:30 4 x 50 IMO @ :45/:50 (1:00) 6 x 50 w/fins Fast kick dolphin @ 1:00 1 x 400 w/fins dolphin on back

WEEK 21	Fri Jan 19 2024
WARMUP	3 x 200 Free 1 x 100 Kick Fly 3 x 100 Freestyle 2 x 100 Paddle w/Pull Buoy @ 2:30/2:40 4 x 100 Pull @ 1:30 4 x 75 Stroke (long underwater on each wall) @ 1:20 4 x 50 25 build to top speed, 25 easy @ 1:00
SPRINT	3 x 200 Best Average @ 3:00/3:10 4 x 50 Avg. Best time@ 1:00 2 x 50's max for time

DISTANCE	3 x { @ 12:00
	   1 x 200 @ 3:00 Dive
	   Go 500 Pace
	   2 x 100 @ 1:40
	   Goal going out 200 pace for 500
	   1 x 100 Dive MAX
	}
	10 x 50 @ 1:00
	Odds 50 Kick
	Evens 50 Swim

MID-DISTANCE	Mile MAX for time 2 x 400 Paddle w/Pull Buoy

WEEK 21	Sat Jan 20 2024

WARMUP	4 x 300 Free-Kick-RIMO – (50 Swim / 50 Drill)
	
	2 x {
	   4 x 50 Fist Drill @ 1:10
	   2 x 25 Build to Pink @ :30
	}

MAIN SET	IM 8 x 200 IMO @ :30 rest 2 x 200 IM @ 2:50 Pink-Red (2:00) 4 x 200 @ :20 rest #1 IM (50 drill/50 swim Pink) #2 RIMO (50 Kick Red no board/50 Swim) 4 x 100 IMO @ 1:30 Pink-Red-Blue-MAX

Monday	Tuesday	Wednesday	Thursday	Friday	Saturday
1 x 200 BackStroke 1 x 200 Fly 1 x 200 Free 1 x 200 Breast 1 x 200 kick 8 x 100 (25 Build/50 Pink/25 Build to Fast Finish) @ 1:40 8 x 50 @ 1:00 #1-3 (1/2 underwater Kick + breakout on each wall) #4-6 Build max of 3 breaths #7-8 DPS SPRINT 10 x 50 @ 4:00 #1-3 MAX of 3 Breaths #4-6 MAX of 2 Breaths #7-9 MAX of 1 Breath #10 No Breath 4 x (75+ 25 white) Descend 8 x (50 + 50 white) Round 1 all red Round 2 all MAX DISTANCE 8 x 200 2 white, 2 pink, 2 red, 2 blue@ 2:30/2:40 9 x 100 3 white, 3 pink, 3 red @ 1:20/1:30 (1:00) 4 x 100 /50 Red/50 White! @ 1:50 Cooldown – 4 x 100 choice @ 1:40 MID-DISTANCE 8 x 100 IM @ 1:20/1:30 4 x 100 fly or free build to no breath/RED finish @ 1:20/1:30 4 x 50 Best Average @ :40/:50 4 x 200 IM @ 2:30/2:40 4 x 100 fly or free build @ 1:20/1:30 4 x 50 Best Average @ :40/:50 4 x 100 JMI @ 1:10 (2:00) 4 x 50 @ :30/:35 10 x 50 @ 1:00 Odds 50 Kick Evens 50 Swim	1 x 500 (250 Free/200 Non-Free/50 BK) 1 x 400 (200 Kick/200 Kick no board) 1 x 200 RIMO 1 x 600 Paddle/Pull Bp 5 by 100's work on great turns 1 x 400 8 x 100 w/fins @ 1:30 8 x 75 IMO @ 1:30 ex: #1-2 50 Fly Build + 25 back MAX 4 x (IMO 2 x 100 @ 1:10/1:20 1 x 200 Drill @ :30 rest 4 x (50 + 50 white) Add up to Best time 200)	3 x 600 #1 200 RIMO/200 Swim/200 Drill #2 300 (50 drill/50 swim best Stroke/300 kick) #3 Swim Choice 8 x 50 @ 1:00 odds: fast turns evens: build to fast finish SPRINT 3 x 300 @ 4:00 (2) White – (1) Pink 6 x 50's MAX for time From Dive @ 5:00 DISTANCE 8 x 50 (25 Drill/ 25 build to max finish) @ :50 1 x 100 Broken @ 25's 2 x 50 MAX 4 x 25 MAX 8 x 200 (free/kick/non-free/drill) @ 2:40 6 x 100 (Back/free/choice) @ +:10 MID-DISTANCE 1 x 1650 Broken 200 White @ :10 rest 300 (150 Pink-150 Red) @ :10 rest 200 Red @ :10 rest 300 (Build to Blue) @ :10 rest 5 x 100 Best Avg @ :10 rest 150 MAX 3 x 200 MAX @ 6:00	200 SKIMPS 8 x 50 @ 1:00 odds: RB.1 evens: RB.3 5 x 50 Dolphin on Back @ :50 12 x 75 Continuous IM @ 1:10 4 x 25 IMO Descend @ :30 SPRINT 4 x 200 Kick white @ 3:30 Paddle/Pull 1 x 400 white @ :10 1 x 300 pink @ :10 1 x 200 red @ :10 4 x 100 Free/Back @ 1:20/1:25 4 x 200 Free/Back @ 3:00 /3:30 Cooldown – 5 x 100 @ 1:40	4 x 200 IM 3 x 100 Freestyle 1 x 200 Kick 6 x 100 DPS @ :50 SPRINT 2 x 200 (100 White/100 Red) @ 3:00/3:10 2 x 200 (100 Pink/100 Red) @ 3:00/3:10 2 x (2 x 100 JMI @ 1:40 4 x 50 Red @ 1:05/1:10/1:15 8 x 25 Max @ 1:00 odds: from Dive evens: from Push) 4 x 100 Descend to MAX @ 1:20/1:40 DISTANCE/MID-DISTANCE 8 x 100 IM @ 1:20/1:30 4 x 75 FL or FR Build/MAX finish last 12.5 @ 1:00 4 x 25 MAX kick to 15m @ :30 4 x 200 IM @ 2:35/2:40 4 x 50 FR or FL Build/MAX last 25 @ 1:00 4 x 25 MAX kick to 15m @ :25 4 x 100 JMI @ 1:00/1:05 (2:00) 4 x 50 @ :30/:35 10 x 50 @ 1:00 Odds 50 Kick Evens 50 Swim	400 RIMO 6 x 100 Non-Free (50 Kick/50 Swim) @ :10 rest 2 x (x 50 fist drill @ 1:00 6 x 25 Build @ :30) 8 x 75 w/fins @ :55 Continuous IM (BR-dolphin kick), Work under waters - easy swim (:30) 4 x 50 IMO @ :50 25 underwater/25 swim (1:00) 9 x 100 w/fins @ 1:20/1:30 4 x 150 Paddles/Fins @ 1:50 IM 2 x 300 (75 IMO) @ 4:10/4:15 4 x 150 (50 back/100 Breast) @ 2:15/2:20 4 x 150 (50 BR/100 Free) @ 2:05/2:10

WEEK 22	Mon Jan 22 2024
WARMUP	1 x 200 BackStroke 1 x 200 Fly 1 x 200 Free 1 x 200 Breast 1 x 200 kick 8 x 100 (25 Build/50 Pink/25 Build to Fast Finish) @ 1:40 8 x 50 @ 1:00 #1-3 (1/2 underwater Kick + breakout on each wall) #4-6 Build max of 3 breaths #7-8 DPS
SPRINT	10 x 50 @ 4:00 #1-3 MAX of 3 Breaths #4-6 MAX of 2 Breaths #7-9 MAX of 1 Breath #10 No Breath 4 x (75+ 25 white) Descend 8 x (50 + 50 white) Round 1 all red Round 2 all MAX
DISTANCE	8 x 200 2 white, 2 pink, 2 red, 2 blue@ 2:30/2:40 (1:00) 9 x 100 3 white, 3 pink, 3 red @ 1:20/1:30 (1:00) 4 x 100 (50 Red/50 White) @ 1:50 Cooldown – 4 x 100 choice @ 1:40
MID-DISTANCE	8 x 100 IM @ 1:20/1:30 4 x 100 fly or free build to no breath/RED finish @ 1:20/1:30 4 x 50 Best Average @ :40/:50 4 x 200 IM @ 2:30/2:40 4 x 100 fly or free build @ 1:20/1:30 4 x 50 Best Average @ :40/:50 4 x 100 JMI @ 1:10 (2:00) 4 x 50 @ :30/:35 10 x 50 @ 1:00 Odds 50 Kick Evens 50 Swim

WEEK 22	Tue Jan 23 2024
WARMUP	1 x 500 (250 Free/200 Non-Free/50 BK) 1 x 400 (200 Kick/200 Kick no board) 1 x 200 RIMO 1 x 600 Paddle/Pull Bp 5 by 100's work on great turns 1 x 400
MAIN SET	8 x 100 w/fins @ 1:30 8 x 75 IMO @ 1:30 ex: #1-2 50 Fly Build + 25 back MAX 4 x { IMO 2 x 100 @ 1:10/1:20 1 x 200 Drill @ :30 rest 4 x (50 + 50 white) Add up to Best time 200 }

WEEK 22	Wed Jan 24 2024

WARMUP	3 x 600
	
	   #1 200 RIMO/200 Swim/200 Drill
	   #2 300 (50 drill/50 swim best Stroke/300 kick)
	#3 Swim Choice
	
	8 x 50 @ 1:00
	odds: fast turns
	evens: build to fast finish

SPRINT	3 x 300 @ 4:00 (2) White – (1) Pink 6 x 50's MAX for time From Dive @ 5:00
DISTANCE	8 x 50 (25 Drill/ 25 build to max finish) @ :50 1 x 100 Broken @ 25's 2 x 50 MAX 4 x 25 MAX 8 x 200 (free/kick/non-free/drill) @ 2:40 6 x 100 (Back/free/choice) @ + :10
MID-DISTANCE	1 x 1650 Broken 200 White @ :10 rest 300 (150 Pink-150 Red) @ :10 rest 200 Red @ :10 rest 300 (Build to Blue) @ :10 rest 5 x 100 Best Avg @ :10 rest 150 MAX 3 x 200 MAX @ 6:00

WEEK 22	Tue Jan 23 2024
WARMUP	1 x 500 (250 Free/200 Non-Free/50 BK) 1 x 400 (200 Kick/200 Kick no board) 1 x 200 RIMO 1 x 600 Paddle/Pull Bp 5 by 100's work on great turns 1 x 400
MAIN SET	8 x 100 w/fins @ 1:30 8 x 75 IMO @ 1:30 ex: #1-2 50 Fly Build + 25 back MAX 4 x { IMO 2 x 100 @ 1:10/1:20 1 x 200 Drill @ :30 rest 4 x (50 + 50 white) Add up to Best time 200 }

WEEK 22	Wed Jan 24 2024

WARMUP	3 x 600
	   #1 200 RIMO/200 Swim/200 Drill
	   #2 300 (50 drill/50 swim best Stroke/300 kick)
	#3 Swim Choice
	
	8 x 50 @ 1:00
	odds: fast turns
	evens: build to fast finish

SPRINT	3 x 300 @ 4:00 (2) White – (1) Pink 6 x 50's MAX for time From Dive @ 5:00
DISTANCE	8 x 50 (25 Drill/ 25 build to max finish) @ :50 1 x 100 Broken @ 25's 2 x 50 MAX 4 x 25 MAX 8 x 200 (free/kick/non-free/drill) @ 2:40 6 x 100 (Back/free/choice) @ + :10
MID-DISTANCE	1 x 1650 Broken 200 White @ :10 rest 300 (150 Pink-150 Red) @ :10 rest 200 Red @ :10 rest 300 (Build to Blue) @ :10 rest 5 x 100 Best Avg @ :10 rest 150 MAX 3 x 200 MAX @ 6:00

WEEK 22	Thu Jan 25 2024
WARMUP	200 SKIMPS 8 x 50 @ 1:00 odds: RB:1 evens: RB:3 5 x 50 Dolphin on Back @ :50 12 x 75 Continuous IM @ 1:10 4 x 25 IMO Descend @ :30 4 x 200 Kick white @ 3:30
MAIN SET	Paddle/Pull 1 x 400 white @ :10 1 x 300 pink @ :10 1 x 200 red @ :10 4 x 100 Free/Back @ 1:20/1:25 4 x 200 Free/Back @ 3:00 /3:30 Cooldown – 5 x 100 @ 1:40

WEEK 22	Fri Jan 26 2024
WARMUP	4 x 200 IM 3 x 100 Freestyle 1 x 200 Kick 6 x 100 DPS @ :50

SPRINT	2 x 200 (100 White / 100 Red) @ 3:00 / 3:10
	2 x 200 (100 Pink / 100 Red) @ 3:00 / 3:10
	
	2 x {
	    2 x 100 JMI @ 1:40
	    4 x 50 Red @ 1:05 / 1:10 / 1:15
	    8 x 25 Max @ 1:00
	    odds: from Dive
	    evens: from Push
	}
	4 x 100 Descend to MAX @ 1:20 / 1:40

DISTANCE/MID-DISTANCE	8 x 100 IM @ 1:20 / 1:30 4 x 75 FL or FR Build / MAX finish last 12.5 @ 1:00 4 x 25 MAX kick to 15m @ :30 4 x 200 IM @ 2:35 / 2:40 4 x 50 FR or FL Build / MAX last 25 @ 1:00 4 x 25 MAX kick to 15m @ :25 4 x 100 JMI @ 1:00 / 1:05 (2:00) 4 x 50 @ :30 / :35 10 x 50 @ 1:00 Odds 50 Kick Evens 50 Swim 6 x 200 @ 6:00

WEEK 22	Sat Jan 27 2024

WARMUP	400 RIMO
	6 x 100 Non-Free (50 Kick/50 Swim) @ :10 rest
	
	2 x {
	  x 50 fist drill @ 1:00
	  6 x 25 Build @ :30
	}
	
	    8 x 75 w/fins @ :55
	    Continuous IM (BR-dolphin kick), Work under waters - easy swim
	    (:30)
	    4 x 50 IMO @ :50
	    25 underwater/25 swim
	    (1:00)
	
	9 x 100 w/fins @ 1:20/1:30
	4 x 150 Paddles/Fins @ 1:50

MAIN SET	IM 2 x 300 (75 IMO) @ 4:10/4:15 4 x 150 (50 back/100 Breast) @ 2:15/2:20 4 x 150 (50 BR/100 Free) @ 2:05/2:10

Monday	Tuesday	Wednesday	Thursday	Friday	Saturday

3 x 300
#1 White/Pink @ 3:50/3:55
#2 (50 Pink/50 max of 4 breaths) @ 4:00
#3 No Breath in or out of walls
 	
10 x 25 w/ chutes @ :45 Red
10 x 25 x/ fins MAX underwater kick @ :30
2 x {
4 x 200 @ 2:30
(1:00)
}
 	
SPRINT
5 x 100 @ 1:20 (no breath in or out of walls) @ 1:30
4 x 25 (Drill/Build/Drill/Sprint) @ :40
 	
3 x 200
100 Swim-100 Kick red
(1:00)
6 x 100
odds: Pink
evens: Red
 	
DISTANCE
4 x 100 IM @ 1:50 Pink
12 x 50 Fins @ :40
4 x 50 #1 drill, #2 build, #3 drill, #4 sprint @ :30
3 x { ~ 2 Minutes between each round
300 White @ 3:50/4:00
2 x 75 Pink @ 1:10/1:15
4 x 100 Red @ 1:10/1:15
2 x 25 MAX @ :40
}
 	
MID-DISTANCE
1 x 800 Paddle/Pull BP: 3-5-7 by 100s
8 x 100 Build to MAX last 25 @ 1:30/1:40
 	
3 x {
400 White 4:40/4:50
2 x 100 Pink @ 1:30/1:40
4 x 100 Red @ 1:05/1:10
2 x 50 MAX @ 1:00
(2:00)
}
	600 Free
	6 x 100 IM D1-3 and 4-6 @ 1:30
	
	10 x 100 (25 drill/50 swim/25 drill) @ 1:30
	
	1 x 200 Kick MAX for time @ 4:00
	4 x 50 kick easy @ 1:10
	1 x 100 Kick MAX for time (dolphin on back)
	2 x {
	
	3 x 400 IM @ :20
	#1 50 Kick RED/50 Swim White
	#2 Descend each 100 + 1/2 way under water MAX kick
	#3 Descend 100's #1-3 to Pink, 4th 100 long streamline fast legs
	2 x {
	12 x 50
	#1-6 Best Stroke @ :45/:55
	#7-12 Worst Stroke @ :50/:55
	}
	6 x 75 w/chutes (2)Fly-(2)Back-(2)Breast @ 1:20 Work under waters
	4 x 100 Free w/fins JMI @ :55/1:00
		400 Back
		200 Free
		200 Kick
		
		2 x {
		4 x 50 fist drill @ 1:00
		4 x 25 build @ :30
		}
		8 x 50 kick @ 1:00
		D1-4 , 5-8 to MAX (start at Pink)
		
		SPRINT
		1 x 500
		odd 100's: Free
		even 100's: Build Kick
		
		5 x 200 @ 2:40
		D1-5
		(2:00)
		12 x 50 JMI @ :35/:45
		2 x 300 (150 White/Build) @ 4:00
		
		DISTANCE
		1 x 800
		(200 Pull/ 200 Swim/ 200 Pull/ 200 IM)
		(1:00)
		4 x 200 @ 2:20/2:40
		Pink-Red-Blue-MAX
		
		10 x 100
		odds: Hold 500 goal pace @ 1:30
		evens: White @ 1:35/1:40
		2 x {
		8 x 50 @ :55
		(:30)
		4 x 25 underwater @ :45
		}
		
		MID-DISTANCE
		5 x 100 Neg Split (Clear-Pink) @ 1:20
		Work long turns
		
		5 x 200 BEST AVERAGE @ 2:20/2:30
		10 x 100 BEST AVERAGE @ 1:30
		4 x 50 MAX @ 1:00
		
		1 x 200 easy
		
		4 x 50 kick MAX @ 1:00
			400 IM
			8 x 50 Kick @ :10 rest
			10 x 100 @ :15 rest
			Odds: Breast
			Evens: Free
			
			1 x 300 (150 kick no board/ 150 Swim) @ 5:30
			1 x 500 white
			2 x 300 Pull @ 3:45/4:00
			10 x 50 @ 1:00
			Odds 50 Free
			Evens 50 Non Free
			
			5 x 100 @ 1:25/1:30
			Descend 1-5
			
			2 x {
			4 x 100
			odds: Free @ 1:50
			evens: Non-Free – Pink @ 1:50/2:00
			4 x 50 @ :40
			}
				9 x 100 @ 1:15 BP: 3-5
				2 x 8 x 50 (25 Drill/ 25 build to max finish) @ :50
				6 x 100 Kick w/fins @ 1:20/1:30
				25 underwater kick/25 dolphin on back/50 kick choice
				
				SPRINT
				4 x 200 Paddle w/Pull Buoy @ 2:40
				#1 Descend each 100
				#2 Build each 200
				#3 Fast Flips
				#4 DPS
				
				8 x (100 + 50 white)
				D1-4 , D5-8
				
				1 x 400 FR/Non-FR by 100
				8 x 50 (2 white/ 2 pink/ 2 red/ 2 pink) @ :50
				4 x 50 Worst Stroke @ 1:00
				
				1 x 300 (50 BK/50 BR)
				3 x 100 (2) Pink (1) Red @ 1:20
				3 x 50 (25 underwater/25 white) @ 1:00
				
				1 x 200 (FR/Non-FR by 100)
				2 x 100 (1) Red (1) Blue @ 1:20
				2 x 50 #1 Stroke Drill @ 1:00
				
				8 x 50 Kick MAX @ 1:00
				
				DISTANCE
				5 x 200 @ 2:40
				1 white, 2 pink, 2 red
				12 x 100 @ 1:25
				6 pink, 6 red
				12 x 50 @ :50
				6 Red, 6 MAX
				
				1 x 200 Kick easy @ 4:00
				4 x 50 Kick MAX @ 1:00
				
				MID-DISTANCE
				3 x {
				1 x 200 @ 3:00 Dive
				Go 500 Pace
				2 x 100 @ 1:40 (500 pace)
				1 x 100 Dive MAX
				}
				
				10 x 50 @ 1:00
				Odds 50 Kick
				Evens 50 Swim
					200 SKIMPS
					1 x 500 Kick
					
					1 x 400 Kick White @ 7:00
					1 x 200 Drill
					
					8 x 50 @ 1:00
					#1-4 Descend 1-4
					#5-8 DPS
					
					2 x (10 x 50 KICK @ 1:30) ALL OUT MAX
					
					400 Free @
					4 x 100 (50 Kick/50 Swim) @ 1:40

WEEK 23	Mon Jan 29 2024

WARMUP	3 x 300
	#1 White/Pink @ 3:50/3:55
	#2 (50 Pink/50 max of 4 breaths) @ 4:00
	#3 No Breath in or out of walls
	
	10 x 25 w/ chutes @ :45 Red
	10 x 25 x/ fins MAX underwater kick @ :30
	2 x {
	   4 x 200 @ 2:30
	   (1:00)
	}

SPRINT	5 x 100 @ 1:20 (no breath in or out of walls) @ 1:30 4 x 25 (Drill/Build/Drill/Sprint) @:40 3 x 200 100 Swim-100 Kick red (1:00) 6 x 100 odds: Pink evens: Red
DISTANCE	4 x 100 IM @ 1:50 Pink 12 x 50 Fins @ :40 4 x 50 #1 drill, #2 build, #3 drill, #4 sprint @ :30 3 x { – 2 Minutes between each round 300 White @ 3:50/4:00 2 x 75 Pink @ 1:10/1:15 4 x 100 Red @ 1:10/1:15 2 x 25 MAX @ :40 }

MID-DISTANCE	1 x 800 Paddle/Pull BP: 3-5-7 by 100s
	8 x 100 Build to MAX last 25 @ 1:30/1:40
	
	3 x {
	   400 White @ 4:40/4:50
	   2 x 100 Pink @ 1:30/1:40
	   4 x 100 Red @ 1:05/1:10
	   2 x 50 MAX @ 1:00
	   (2:00)
	}

WEEK 23	Tue Jan 30 2024
WARMUP	600 Free 6 x 100 IM D1-3 and 4-6 @ 1:30 10 x 100 (25 drill/50 swim/25 drill) @ 1:30 1 x 200 Kick MAX for time @ 4:00 4 x 50 kick easy @ 1:10 1 x 100 Kick MAX for time (dolphin on back)

MAIN SET	3 x 400 IM @ :20
	#1 50 Kick RED/50 Swim White
	#2 Descend each 100 + 1/2 way under water MAX kick
	#3 Descend 100's #1-3 to Pink, 4th 100 long streamline fast legs
	2 x {
	   12 x 50
	   #1-6 Best Stroke @ :45/:55
	   #7-12 Worst Stroke @ :50/:55
	}
	6 x 75 w/chutes (2)Fly-(2)Back-(2)Breast @ 1:20 Work under waters
	4 x 100 Free w/fins JMI @ :55/1:00

WEEK 23	Wed Jan 31 2024

WARMUP	400 Back
	200 Free
	200 Kick
	
	2 x {
	    4 x 50 fist drill @ 1:00
	    4 x 25 build @ :30
	}
	8 x 50 Kick @ 1:00
	D1-4 , 5-8 to MAX (start at Pink)

SPRINT	1 x 500 odd 100's: Free even 100's: Build Kick 5 x 200 @ 2:40 D1-5 (2:00) 12 x 50 JMI @ :35/:45 2 x 300 (150 White/Build) @ 4:00

DISTANCE	1 x 800
	(200 Pull/ 200 Swim/ 200 Pull/ 200 IM)
	(1:00)
	4 x 200 @ 2:20/2:40
	Pink-Red-Blue-MAX
	
	10 x 100
	odds: Hold 500 goal pace @ 1:30
	evens: White @ 1:35/1:40
	2 x {
	    8 x 50 @ :55
	    (:30)
	    4 x 25 underwater @ :45
	}

MID-DISTANCE	5 x 100 Neg Split (Clear-Pink) @ 1:20 Work long turns 5 x 200 BEST AVERAGE @ 2:20/2:30 10 x 100 BEST AVERAGE @ 1:30 4 x 50 MAX @ 1:00 1 x 200 easy 4 x 50 kick MAX @ 1:00

WEEK 23	Thu Feb 01 2024
WARMUP	400 IM 8 x 50 Kick @ :10 rest 10 x 100 @ :15 rest Odds: Breast Evens: Free 1 x 300 (150 Kick no board/ 150 Swim) @ 5:30 1 x 500 white 2 x 300 Pull @ 3:45/4:00 10 x 50 @ 1:00 Odds 50 Free Evens 50 Non Free

MAIN SET	5 x 100 @ 1:25/1:30
	Descend 1-5
	
	2 x {
	   4 x 100
	   odds: Free @ 1:50
	   evens: Non-Free – Pink @ 1:50/2:00
	   4 x 50 @ :40
	}

WEEK 23	Fri Feb 02 2024
WARMUP	9 x 100 @ 1:15 BP: 3-5 2 x 8 x 50 (25 Drill/ 25 build to max finish) @ :50 6 x 100 Kick w/fins @ 1:20/1:30 25 underwater kick/25 dolphin on back/50 kick choice 4 x 200 Paddle w/Pull Buoy @ 2:40 #1 Descend each 100 #2 Build each 200 #3 Fast Flips #4 DPS
SPRINT	8 x (100 + 50 white) D1-4 , D5-8 1 x 400 FR/Non-FR by 100 8 x 50 (2 white/ 2 pink/ 2 red/ 2 pink) @ :50 4 x 50 Worst Stroke @ 1:00 1 x 300 (50 BK/50 BR) 3 x 100 (2) Pink (1) Red @ 1:20 3 x 50 (25 underwater/25 white) @ 1:00 1 x 200 (FR/Non-FR by 100) 2 x 100 (1) Red (1) Blue @ 1:20 2 x 50 #1 Stroke Drill @ 1:00 8 x 50 Kick MAX @ 1:00
DISTANCE	5 x 200 @ 2:40 1 white, 2 pink, 2 red 12 x 100 @ 1:25 6 pink, 6 red 12 x 50 @ :50 6 Red, 6 MAX 1 x 200 Kick easy @ 4:00 4 x 50 Kick MAX @ 1:00

MID-DISTANCE	3 x {
	   1 x 200 @ 3:00 Dive
	   Go 500 Pace
	   2 x 100 @ 1:40 (500 pace)
	   1 x 100 Dive MAX
	}
	10 x 50 @ 1:00
	Odds 50 Kick
	Evens 50 Swim

WEEK 23	Sat Feb 03 2024
WARMUP	200 SKIMPS 1 x 500 Kick 1 x 400 Kick White @ 7:00 1 x 200 Drill 8 x 50 @ 1:00 #1-4 Descend 1-4 #5-8 DPS
MAIN SET	2 x (10 x 50 KICK @ 1:30) ALL OUT MAX 400 Free @ 4 x 100 (50 Kick/50 Swim) @ 1:40

FEBRUARY — ELITE SWIM WORKOUT '24 — WEEK 24

Monday	Tuesday	Wednesday	Thursday	Friday	Saturday
1 x 500 Free RB5 3 x 100 Kick 3 x 100 Free RB5	3 x 200 #1 Free #2 (50 BK/50 Breast) #3 DPS Choice	3 x 200 #1 Free #2 (50 BK/50 Breast) #3 DPS Choice	600 (300 Free/300 Non-Free) 400 Free 200 Kick 200 (100 BK/50 Choice/50 kick)	1 x 400 Free 1 x 200 Kick with board 3 x 100 Freestyle	500 Choice 200 IM 8 x 50 Kick @ :10 rest

5 x 50 Dolphin on Back @ :50
12 x 75 Continuous IM @ 1:10
4 x 25 IMO Descend @ :30
	4 x 75 Stroke (long underwater on each wall) @ 1:20
	5 x 100 @ 1:25/1:35
	Keep all the same speed
		2 x {
		100 Drill #1 Stroke @ 1:50
		2 x 75 (White/Pink/Blue) @ 1:10
		2 x 50 @ :35/:450
		2 x 25 underwater kick @ :30
		}
		4 x 150 Kick (White/Pink/Build to MAX finish) @ 2:15
			5 x 50 @ 1:00
			5 x 50 drill same Stroke different drill @ 1:00
			12 x 50 Paddle/Pull @ :45
				3 x 300 @ 3:45/3:55
				8 x 25 Paddles DPS – Count Stroke per 25 @ :45
				4 x 25 Keep Same Stroke Count as w/ paddles per 25
					2 x {
					3 x 50 fist drill @ 1:00
					8 x 25 #1 Stroke drill @ :45
					fly: press/pop, back: catchup, Breast: pull w/ little paddles, Free: single arm
					4 x 25 build @ :30
					}

SPRINT 4 x 200 @ 3:00 (2) White (1) Pink (1:00) 4 x 100 Pink – Red – Blue- MAX @ 1:20 2 x (8 x 50 (2 @ :35, 1 @ :50) (:30) 4 x 25 underwater @ :40 }		**SPRINT** 8 x 50 MAX Turns Mid Pool @ :50 4 x build @ :30 6 x 50 @ 4:00 #1-2 MAX w/ 2 Breaths #3-4 MAX w/ 1 Breath #5-6 MAX w/ 0 Breaths 4 x 25 w/fins from Dive	4 x 400 IM Red 2 min rest in between 1 x 400 cool down	5 x 50 drill @ 1:00 4 x 25 Kick Build each 25 @ :40 4 x 50 Kick Descend @ :55 4 x 25 Kick @ :30 9 x 50 (2 @ :40, 1 @ :30)	4 x 100 (50 #1 Stroke/50 Free) @ 1:30 Stroke – easy free

DISTANCE
1 x (600 + 200 easy) Pink
4 x (300 + 100)
D 1-4 to Pink
4 x (200 + 50 easy)
White-Pink-Red-Red
8 x (100 + 50 easy)
All Red
8 x (50 + 50 easy)
Hold Goal 500 Pace
		DISTANCE
		12 x 75 (2 easy @ 1:10, 1 FAST @ 1:00)
				SPRINT
				5 x {
				100 Best Average @ 2:00
				4 x 50 Avg. Best time 200 Pace @ 1:00 +
				1:00 rest
				}
					1 x Broken 200
					1 x 100 MAX
					2 x 50 MAX

MID-DISTANCE 1 x 900 (300 Fly-300 Free 300 stretch drill) 1 x 600 (300 fl/fr-300 back/breast) 1 x 1000 Broken 9 x 100 @ 1:15 BP: 3-5 (10 x 100 @ :20 rest)		1 x 600 Pull @ 7:00/7:50 4 x 75 Kick @ 1:20 odds: White-Pink-Red Evens: Red-Pink-White (1:00) 1 x 600 Pull @ 6:50/7:40 4 x 100 Kick @ 1:30/1:40 Descend to MAX start @ Pink (2:00) 2 x 500 Swim @ 5:20/5:40 (2:00) 4 x 200 Swim w/fins @ 2:15		**DISTANCE** 4 x 100 MAX KICK @ 1:40 400 Easy 5 x 75 MAX @ 5:00 400 Easy 4 x 100 MAX Kick @ 1:40 4 x 50 MAX @ 3:00	
		MID-DISTANCE 100 Pink 200 (Pink 100 x 2 @ 2:20/2:30 300 (Red 200 + Pink 100) @ 4:00/4:30 400 (Red 300 + Pink 100) @ 5:20/6:00 100 Red 200 (Red 100 x 2) @ 2:20/2:30 300 (Blue 200 + Red 100) @ 4:00/4:30 400 (Blue 300 + Red 100) @ 5:20/6:00		**MID-DISTANCE** 2 x 200 (White/Pink) @ 2:30 4 x 100 Choice @ 1:30 8 x 50 D 1-4, 5-8 @ 1:00 25s from a dive MAX 6 x 25 build to max finish 6 x 100 (Free/Non-Free) @ 1:40	

171

WEEK 24	Mon Feb 05 2024
WARMUP	1 x 500 Free RB5 3 x 100 Kick 3 x 100 Free RB5 5 x 50 Dolphin on Back @ :50 12 x 75 Continuous IM @ 1:10 4 x 25 IMO Descend @ :30
SPRINT	4 x 200 @ 3:00 (2) White (1) Pink (1:00) 4 x 100 Pink – Red – Blue- MAX @ 1:20 2 x { 8 x 50 (2 @ :35, 1 @ :50) (:30) 4 x 25 underwater @ :40 }
DISTANCE	1 x (600 + 200 easy) Pink 4 x (300 + 100) D 1-4 to Pink 4 x (200 + 50 easy) White-Pink-Red-Red 8 x (100 + 50 easy) All Red 8 x (50 + 50 easy) Hold Goal 500 Pace
MID-DISTANCE	1 x 900 (300 Fly-300 Free 300 stretch drill) 1 x 600 (300 fl/fr-300 back/breast) 1 x 1000 Broken 9 x 100 @ 1:15 BP: 3-5 (10 x 100 @ :20 rest)

WEEK 24	Tue Feb 06 2024
WARMUP	3 x 200 #1 Free #2 (50 BK/50 Breast) #3 DPS Choice
MAIN SET	4 x 75 Stroke (long underwater on each wall) @ 1:20 5 x 100 @ 1:25/1:35 Keep all the same speed

WEEK 24	Wed Feb 07 2024

WARMUP	3 x 200
	#1 Free
	#2 (50 BK/50 Breast)
	#3 DPS Choice
	
	2 x {
	   100 Drill #1 Stroke @ 1:50
	   2 x 75 (White/Pink/Blue) @ 1:10
	   2 x 50 @ :35/:450
	   2 x 25 underwater kick @ :30
	}
	4 x 150 Kick (White/Pink/Build to MAX finish) @ 2:15

SPRINT	8 x 50 MAX Turns Mid Pool @ :50 4 x build @ :30 6 x 50 @ 4:00 #1-2 MAX w/ 2 Breaths #3-4 MAX w/ 1 Breath #5-6 MAX w/ 0 Breaths 4 x 25 w/fins from Dive
DISTANCE	12 x 75 (2 easy @ 1:10, 1 FAST @ 1:00) 1 x 600 Pull @ 7:00/7:50 4 x 75 Kick @ 1:20 odds: White-Pink-Red Evens: Red-Pink-White (1:00) 1 x 600 Pull @ 6:50/7:40 4 x 100 Kick @ 1:30/1:40 Descend to MAX start @ Pink (2:00) 2 x 500 Swim @ 5:20/5:40 (2:00) 4 x 200 Swim w/fins @ 2:15
MID-DISTANCE	100 Pink 200 (Pink 100 x 2 @ 2:20/2:30 300 (Red 200 + Pink 100) @ 4:00/4:30 400 (Red 300 + Pink 100) @ 5:20/6:00 100 Red 200 (Red 100 x 2) @ 2:20/2:30 300 (Blue 200 + Red 100) @ 4:00/4:30 400 (Blue 300 + Red 100) @ 5:20/6:00

WEEK 24	Thu Feb 08 2024
WARMUP	600 (300 Free/300 Non-Free) 400 Free 200 Kick 200 (100 BK/50 Choice/50 kick) 5 x 50 @ 1:00 5 x 50 drill same Stroke different drill @ 1:00 12 x 50 Paddle/Pull @ :45
MAIN SET	4 x 400 IM Red 2 min rest in between 1 x 400 cool down

WEEK 24	Fri Feb 09 2024
WARMUP	1 x 400 Free 1 x 200 Kick with board 3 x 100 Freestyle 3 x 300 @ 3:45/3:55 (1:00) 8 x 25 Paddles DPS – Count Stroke per 25 @ :45 4 x 25 Keep Same Stroke Count as w/ paddles per 25 5 x 50 drill @ 1:00 4 x 25 Kick Build each 25 @ :40 4 x 50 Kick Descend @ :55 4 x 25 Kick @ :30 9 x 50 (2 @ :40, 1 @ :30)

SPRINT	5 x {
	   100 Best Average @ 2:00
	   4 x 50 Avg. Best time 200 Pace @ 1:00 + 1:00 rest
	}

DISTANCE	4 x 100 MAX KICK @ 1:40 400 Easy 5 x 75 MAX @ 5:00 400 Easy 4 x 100 MAX Kick @ 1:40 4 x 50 MAX @ 3:00
MID-DISTANCE	2 x 200 (White/Pink) @ 2:30 4 x 100 Choice @ 1:30 8 x 50 D 1-4, 5-8 @ 1:00 25s from a dive MAX 6 x 25 build to max finish 6 x 100 (Free/Non-Free) @ 1:40

WEEK 24	Sat Feb 10 2024

WARMUP	500 Choice
	200 IM
	8 x 50 Kick @ :10 rest
	
	2 x {
	   3 x 50 fist drill @ 1:00
	   8 x 25 #1 Stroke drill @ :45
	   fly: press/pop, back: catchup, Breast: pull w/ little paddles, Free: single arm
	   4 x 25 build @ :30
	}

MAIN SET	4 x 100 (50 #1 Stroke/50 Free) @ 1:30 Stroke – easy free 1 x Broken 200 1 x 100 MAX 2 x 50 MAX

FEBRUARY — ELITE SWIM WORKOUT '24 — WEEK 25

Monday

500 Choice
200 IM
8 x 50 Kick @ :10 rest

2 x {
100 Drill #1 Stroke @ 1:50
2 x 75 (White/Pink/Blue) @ 1:10
2 x 50 @ :35/:450
2 x 25 underwater kick @ :30
}
4 x 150 Kick (White/Pink/Build to MAX finish) @ 2:15

SPRINT
2 x (300 + 100 white)
White-Pink
4 x (50 + 50 white)
All Kick Descend
(2:00)
2 x 300 IM @ 4:20
4 x (100 + 100 white)
All Kick Descend to MAX
(2:00)
8 x 100 @ 1:40
50 Kick/50 Swim
8 x 50 (25 BK/25 Choice)

DISTANCE
5 x (200 Best Average @ 3:10 + 4 x 50 Best
Avg. @ :50 + 1:00 rest)

MID-DISTANCE
2 x 300 Paddle/ @ 3:30/3:40/3:50
White/Descend to Pink

4 x 50 IMO (Drill Fly) @ 1:10
2 x 300 (100 Free/100 Back/100 Breast) @
4 x 50 RIMO (Drill Fly) @ 1:10
6 x 75 @ 1:20
odds: Free/Non-Free/back
evens: back/choice/free

Tuesday

200 SKIMPS
Pull- (2 x 25 Choice/75 Swim)

6 x 50 Fingertip drill @ 1:00
2 x 100 Catch-up drill @ 2:00
2 x 100 Fly Kick

8 x 50 @ 1:00
1st 25: Work on MAX breakout off wall
2nd 25: Work on MAX perfect finish
}
4 x 100 (50 Non-Free/25 back/25 Choice) @
1:50

2 x 200 @ 2:30/2:40
White-Pink
4 x 100 @ 1:10/1:20
Pink-Red-Blue-MAX

4 x 50 @ 1:00
odds: 25 swim/25 underwater
evens: 25 no breath /25 white

Wednesday

4 x 200
#1 Free #2 Back/Breast by 50's #3 100
BK/100 Choice #4 Free

1 x 300 Kick
2 x 200 (100 White/100 Red Kick @ 3:30
6 x 50 D1-3 to Pink, 4-6 to MAX (start at
White) @ 1:00

8 x 50 @ 1:00
Each one work one flip turns pushing off on
back
4 x 100 JMI @ 1:10/1:15
#1-2 Neg Split (White/Red)
#2-4 DPS

SPRINT
8 x 100
odds: Free JMI @ 1:10/1:15
evens: Breast kick @ 1:40
(2:00)
6 x 75 D1-4 , Hold Red on 5-6 @ 120
4 x 50 Ascend at Blue @ 1:00

20 x 25
#1-10 w/ chutes @ :45
#11-20 w/ fins underwater kick @ :30

DISTANCE
4 x 75 Kick @ 1:30
odds: White-Pink-Red
evens: Red-Pink-White
8 x 25 Sprints @ :30
5 x 100 @ 7:00 MAX
1 x 100 w/fins MAX go best time

MID-DISTANCE
5 x 200 Paddle/Pull Pink @ 3:00

4 x 100 IMO @ 1:40
1 x 500 White @ 6:15/6:30
4 x 200 D1-4 @ 2:20
1 x 400 Pink @ 5:00/5:10
4 x 100 D1-4 @ 1:30

Thursday

200 SKIMPS
8 x 50 @ 1:00
odds: RB:1
evens: RB:3

8 x 50 @ 1:00
Each one work one flip turns pushing off on
back
4 x 100 JMI @ 1:10/1:15
#1-2 Neg Split (White/Red)
#2-4 DPS

IM
8 x (50 + 50 white)
Hold 200 Goal Pace
(2:00)
2 x {
200 + 100 white (200 - Neg Split)
100 + 50 white (100 - out pace of 200 + 6
2 x (50 + 50 white) (50 - Last 100 Split of
200 divided by 2)
}
1 x 400 Fin Swim
(1:00)
2 x (100 w/fins + 100 white)
add up to best time 200

Friday

500 Free
6 x 100 IM @ :15 rest
4 x 100 Kick IM Order

8 x 100 @ 1:40
#1-3 (50 Kick Red/50 Kick White)
#4-7 (75 Kick Pink/25 Kick MAX)
#8 100 Kick MAX

SPRINT
1 x 400 Scull

1 x 400 (200 Free-White/200 Non-Free –
White) @ 5:10
6 x 100 Paddle @ 1:15
#1-3 Descend, #4-6 Ascend

300 (150 Non-Free – Pink/150 Free – White)
@ 4:10
4 x 100 Fins @ 1:10
1 x 200 (100 Drill/100 Kick) @ 3:10
4 x 100 JMI @ 1:10/1:20
100 Build each Turn @ 1:30
3 x 100 fast breakouts @ 1:30

DISTANCE
3 x 200 @ 2:20/2:30
8 x (100 Fast + 50 easy)
4 x (50 MAX + 50 easy)

MID-DISTANCE
10 x 75 @ 1:10
#1-5 (easy/medium/fast)
#6-10 IMO + free

4 x (200 pad/pull + 100 easy)
Descend
5 x (100 + 50 easy)
#1-5 Goal 500 Pace
4 x (50 + 50 easy) All FAST

Saturday

600 Free
6 x 100 IM D1-3 and 4-6 @ 1:30
10 x 100 (25 drill/50 swim/25 drill) @ 1:30

8 x 50 @ 1:00
odds: fast turns
evens: build to fast finish

5 x {
200 IM Best Average 2:20/2:40/2:50
4 x 50 IMO @ 1:10
1:00 rest
}

WEEK 25	Mon Feb 12 2024

WARMUP	500 Choice
	200 IM
	8 x 50 Kick @ :10 rest
	
	2 x {
	    100 Drill #1 Stroke @ 1:50
	    2 x 75 (White/Pink/Blue) @ 1:10
	    2 x 50 @ :35/:450
	    2 x 25 underwater kick @ :30
	}
	4 x 150 Kick (White/Pink/Build to MAX finish) @ 2:15

SPRINT	2 x (300 + 100 white) White-Pink 4 x (50 + 50 white) All Kick Descend (2:00) 2 x 300 IM @ 4:20 4 x (100 + 100 white) All Kick Descend to MAX (2:00) 8 x 100 @ 1:40 50 Kick/50 Swim 8 x 50 (25 BK/25 Choice)

DISTANCE	5 x {
	200 Best Average @ 3:10
	4 x 50 Best Avg. @ :50
	1:00 rest
	}

MID-DISTANCE	2 x 300 Paddle/ @ 3:30/3:40/3:50 White/Descend to Pink 4 x 50 IMO (Drill Fly) @ 1:10 2 x 300 (100 Free/100 Back/100 Breast) @ 4 x 50 RIMO (Drill Fly) @ 1:10 6 x 75 @ 1:20 odds: Free/Non-Free/back evens: back/choice/free

WEEK 25	Tue Feb 13 2024
WARMUP	200 SKIMPS Pull- (2 x 25 Choice/75 Swim) 6 x 50 Fingertip drill @ 1:00 4 x 100 Catch-up drill @ 2:00 2 x 100 Fly Kick 8 x 50 @ 1:00 1st 25: Work on MAX breakout off wall 2nd 25: Work on MAX perfect finish 2 x 200 @ 2:30/2:40 White-Pink
MAIN SET	4 x 100 @ 1:10/1:20 Pink-Red-Blue-MAX 4 x 50 @ 1:00 odds: 25 swim/25 underwater evens: 25 no breath /25 white 4 x 100 (50 Non-Free/25 back/25 Choice) @ 1:50

WEEK 25	Wed Feb 14 2024
WARMUP	4 x 200 #1 Free #2 Back/Breast by 50's #3 100 BK/100 Choice #4 Free 1 x 300 Kick 2 x 200 (100 White/100 Red Kick @ 3:30 6 x 50 D1-3 to Pink, 4-6 to MAX (start at White) @ 1:00 8 x 50 @ 1:00 Each one work one flip turns pushing off on back 4 x 100 JMI @ 1:10/1:15 #1-2 Neg Split (White/Red) #2-4 DPS
SPRINT	8 x 100 odds: Free JMI @ 1:10/1:15 evens: Breast kick @ 1:40 (2:00) 6 x 75 D1-4 , Hold Red on 5-6 @ 1:20 4 x 50 Ascend at Blue @ 1:00 20 x 25 #1-10 w/ chutes @ :45 #11-20 w/ fins underwater kick @ :30
DISTANCE	4 x 75 Kick @ 1:30 odds: White-Pink-Red evens: Red-Pink-White 8 x 25 Sprints @ :30 5 x 100 @ 7:00 MAX 1 x 100 w/fins MAX go best time
MID-DISTANCE	5 x 200 Paddle/Pull Pink@ 3:00 4 x 100 IMO @ 1:40 1 x 500 White @ 6:15/6:30 4 x 200 D 1-4 @ 2:20 1 x 400 Pink @ 5:00/5:10 4 x 100 D 1-4 @ 1:30

WEEK 25	Thu Feb 15 2024
WARMUP	200 SKIMPS 8 x 50 @ 1:00 odds: RB:1 evens: RB:3 8 x 50 @ 1:00 Each one work one flip turns pushing off on back 4 x 100 JMI @ 1:10/1:15 #1-2 Neg Split (White/Red) #2-4 DPS

MAIN SET	IM
	8 x (50 + 50 white)
	Hold 200 Goal Pace
	(2:00)
	2 x {
	   200 + 100 white (200 - Neg Split)
	   100 + 50 white (100 - out pace of 200 + 6
	   2 x (50 + 50 white) (50 - Last 100 Split of 200 divided by 2)
	}
	1 x 400 Fin Swim
	(1:00)
	2 x (100 w/fins + 100 white)
	add up to best time 200

WEEK 25	Fri Feb 16 2024
WARMUP	500 Free 6 x 100 IM @ :15 rest 4 x 100 Kick IM Order 8 x 100 @ 1:40 #1-3 (50 Kick Red/50 Kick White) #4-7 (75 Kick Pink/25 Kick MAX) #8 100 Kick MAX
SPRINT	1 x 400 Scull 1 x 400 (200 Free-White/200 Non-Free – White) @ 5:10 6 x 100 Paddle @ 1:15 #1-3 Descend, #4-6 Ascend 300 (150 Non-Free – Pink/150 Free – White) @ 4:10 4 x 100 Fins @ 1:10 1 x 200 (100 Drill/100 Kick) @ 3:10 4 x 100 JMI @ 1:10/1:20 100 Build each Turn @ 1:30 3 x 100 fast breakouts @ 1:30
DISTANCE	3 x 200 @ 2:20/2:30 8 x (100 Fast + 50 easy) 4 x (50 MAX + 50 easy)
MID-DISTANCE	10 x 75 @ 1:10 #1-5 (easy/medium/fast) #6-10 IMO + free 4 x (200 pad/pull + 100 easy) Descend 5 x (100 + 50 easy) #1-5 Goal 500 Pace 4 x (50 + 50 easy) All FAST

WEEK 25	Sat Feb 17 2024
WARMUP	600 Free 6 x 100 IM D1-3 and 4-6 @ 1:30 10 x 100 (25 drill/50 swim/25 drill) @ 1:30 8 x 50 @ 1:00 odds: fast turns evens: build to fast finish

MAIN SET	5 x {
	   200 IM Best Average 2:20/2:40/2:50
	   4 x 50 IMO @ 1:10
	   1:00 rest
	}

Monday	Tuesday	Wednesday	Thursday	Friday	Saturday

200 SKIMPS
6 x 50 IMO @ 1:00
 	
8 x 50 @ :50
odds: build into first wall, great turn
evens: build into finish, great finish
 	
2 x {
  4 x 25 (drill,build,drill,MAX) @ :40
}
 	
SPRINT
 	
6 x 100 w/fins (25 kick/50 swim/25 dolphin on back) @ 1:40
 	
2 x 300 White @ 4:00
4 x 50 D1-4 @ 1:00
2 x 200 White @ 2:40
4 x 50 D1-4 @ 1:00
2 x 100 White @ 1:40
4 x 50 Max Breakout @ 1:40
 	
DISTANCE
 	
10 x (50 + 50 easy)
500 Hold 500 Goal Pace –1
200 Hold 200 Goal Pace
5 x (100 + 100 easy)
500 – Hold 500 Goal Pace
200 – Hold 200 Goal Pace + 2
3 x (200 + 100 easy)
D1-3
 	
MID-DISTANCE
 	
5 x 200 2 white, 2 pink, 1 red@ 2:40 (1:00)
8 x 150 2 white, 2 pink, 2 red, 2 blue@ 2:00 (1:00)
10 x 100 2 white, 2 pink, 2 red, 2 blue 2 MAX@ 1:45
 	
4 x 100 choice @ 1:40
	3 x 300
	#1 Free
	#2 Back
	
	6 x 200
	#1-2 (100 Back/100 Breast) @ +20 rest
	#3-4 Choice Swim @ 2:40
	#5-6 (50 BK/100 Kick no board/50 Choice)
	
	IM
	
	3 x (200 + 50 white) build 4th 25 to MAX transition turn + 5 Strokes breakout
	#1 (100 Fly/100 Back)
	#2 (100 Back/100 Breast)
	#3 (100 Breast/100 Free)
	
	4 x (75 IMO Pink + 50 Red next Stroke)
	
	4 x (25 Blue IMO Pink + w/ blue transition turn + 50 pink)
	ex. Round 1 - 25 blue fly + 50 pink back work transition turn and breakout
	
	6 x 50 (25 kick MAX Dolphin underwater/25 swim) w/fins
		8 x 125
		odds: 25 Free/50 Kick no board/50 Non-Free
		evens: 50 Free/75 Kick
		
		1 x 200 Scull on Back
		1 x 200 Scull on Front
		
		10 x 50 (Kick/Drill) @ :55
		1 x 400 Paddle/Fins
		4 x 25 sprint kick @ :50
		
		SPRINT
		
		12 x 25 @ :45
		10 x 50 MAX @ 4:00
		#1-3 max of 3 breaths
		#4-6 max of 2 breaths
		#7-9 max of 1 breath
		#10 No Breath
		
		300 white
		
		DISTANCE
		
		2 x 400 Paddle w/Pull Buoy @ 4:45/5:00
		3 x 200 IM :30 sec
		4 x 50 Free @ :40
		
		2 x 300 (150 Free/150 Non-Free) @ 4:00
		4 x 100 Descend @ 1:30
		4 x 50 Free @ :40
		
		MID-DISTANCE
		
		1 x 800 White
		4 x 200 descend each 200 @ 2:40 (2:00)
		8 x 100 JMI @ 1:10/1:15
		4 x 100 @ 1:35
		4 x 75 Build @ 1:00
			1 x 400 (200 Free/200 Back)
			1 x 300 (150 Kick non-free/150 kick breast)
			1 x 200 (100 BK/100 Choice)
			1 x 100 IM
			
			8 x 100 (25 Build/50 Pink/25 Build to Fast Finish) @ 1:40
			8 x 50 @ 1:00
			#1-3 (1/2 underwater Kick + breakout on each wall)
			#4-6 Build max of 3 breaths
			#7-8 DPS
			
			8 x 200 @ 2:40
			#1 (25 Red + 175 White)
			#2 (50 Red + 150 White)
			#3 (75 Red + 125 White)
			#4 (100 Red + 100 White)
			#5 (125 Blue + 75 White)
			#6 (150 Blue + 50 White)
			#7 (175 Blue + 25 White)
			#8 200 MAX
			
			1 x 400 (50 Free/50 Non-Free)
			8 x 50 KICK D1-4, 5-8 to MAX @ 1:00
				4 x 200
				IM-Non-Free-Free-Kick
				6 x 25 Build @ :30
				
				SPRINT
				
				3 x 200 Free @ 2:30 D1-3
				4 x (100 red + 50 white)
				4 x (50 MAX + 50 white)
				
				DISTANCE
				
				4 x {
				  1 x 75 MAX (:30)
				  50 MAX from push
				}
				
				1 x 300 Easy
				2 x 200 @ 2:30
				White-Pink
				8 x 25 w/fins Underwater @ :40
				
				MID-DISTANCE
				
				4 x 200
				#1-2 IM Descend, #2-4 Ascend Free
				
				6 x 200 @ 2:30/2:50
				#1-2 200 Pink – 25 Blue
				#3-4 200 Red – 25 MAX
				#5-6 200 Red – 25 Red max of 2 breaths
				
				10 x (100 + 50 easy)
				Goal 1000 Pace
				10 x (50 + 50 easy)
				Goal 500 Pace
					1 x 600 (300 Free-300 NonFree)
					4 x 100 IMO (drill fly) @ :10 rest
					8 x 50 (Fly/Free, Back/Free, Breast/Free, Free/Free) @
					
					6 x 75 (Kick/drill/swim) @ 1:10
					8 x 25 @ :30
					odds: drill/ evens: stroke
					
					3 x 400 IM w/fins Fly & Free - BP- 3,5 by 50 @ 6:30
					
					3 x 100 Fly/Back/BR @ 1:20
					
					2 x {
					  3 x 200 Paddle w/Pull Buoy
					  6 x 100 @ 1:05/1:10/1:15
					}

WEEK 26	Mon Feb 19 2024

WARMUP	200 SKIMPS
	6 x 50 IMO @ 1:00
	
	8 x 50 @ :50
	odds: build into first wall, great turn
	evens: build into finish, great finish
	
	2 x {
	   4 x 25 (drill,build,drill,MAX) @ :40
	}

SPRINT	6 x 100 w/fins (25 kick/50 swim/25 dolphin on back) @ 1:40 2 x 300 White @ 4:00 4 x 50 D 1-4 @ 1:00 2 x 200 White @ 2:40 4 x 50 D 1-4 @ 1:00 2 x 100 White @ 1:40 4 x 50 Max Breakout @ 1:40
DISTANCE	10 x (50 + 50 easy) 500 Hold 500 Goal pace −1 200 Hold 200 Goal Pace 5 x (100 + 100 easy) 500 − Hold 500 Goal Pace 200 − Hold 200 Goal Pace + 2 3 x (200 + 100 easy) Descend 1-3
MID-DISTANCE	5 x 200 2 white, 2 pink, 1 red@ 2:40 (1:00) 8 x 150 2 white, 2 pink, 2 red, 2 blue@ 2:00 (1:00) 10 x 100 2 white, 2 pink, 2 red, 2 blue 2 MAX@ 1:45 4 x 100 choice @ 1:40

WEEK 26	Tue Feb 20 2024
WARMUP	3 x 300 #1 Free #2 Back #2 (150 Kick / 150 Swim choice) 6 x 200 #1-2 (100 Back / 100 Breast) @ +:20 rest #3-4 Choice Swim @ 2:40 #5-6 (50 BK / 100 Kick no board / 50 Choice)
MAIN SET	IM 3 x (200 + 50 white) build 4th 25 to MAX transition turn + 5 Strokes breakout #1 (100 Fly / 100 Back) #2 (100 Back / 100 Breast) #3 (100 Breast / 100 Free) 4 x (75 IMO Pink + 50 Red next Stroke) 4 x (25 Blue IMO w/ blue transition turn + 50 pink) ex. Round 1 - 25 blue fly + 50 pink back work transition turn and breakout 6 x 50 (25 kick MAX Dolphin underwater / 25 swim) w/ fins

WEEK 26	Wed Feb 21 2024
WARMUP	8 x 125 odds: 25 Free/50 Kick no board/50 Non-Free evens: 50 Free/75 Kick 1 x 200 Scull on Back 1 x 200 Scull on Front 10 x 50 (Kick/Drill) @ :55 1 x 400 Paddle/Fins 4 x 25 sprint kick @ :50
SPRINT	12 x 25 @ :45 10 x 50 MAX @ 4:00 #1-3 max of 3 breaths #4-6 max of 2 breaths #7-9 max of 1 breath #10 No Breath 300 white
DISTANCE	2 x 400 Paddle w/Pull Buoy @ 4:45/5:00 3 x 200 IM :30 sec 4 x 50 Free @ :40 2 x 300 (150 Free/150 Non-Free) @ 4:00 4 x 100 Descend @ 1:30 4 x 50 Free @ :40
MID-DISTANCE	1 x 800 White 4 x 200 descend each 200 @ 2:40 (2:00) 8 x 100 JMI @ 1:10/1:15 4 x 100 @ 1:35 (1:00) 4 x 75 Build @ 1:00

WEEK 26	Thu Feb 22 2024
WARMUP	1 x 400 (200 Free/200 Back) 1 x 300 (150 Kick non-free/150 kick breast) 1 x 200 (100 BK/100 Choice) 1 x 100 IM 8 x 100 (25 Build/50 Pink/25 Build to Fast Finish) @ 1:40 8 x 50 @ 1:00 #1-3 (1/2 underwater Kick + breakout on each wall) #4-6 Build max of 3 breaths #7-8 DPS
MAIN SET	8 x 200 @ 2:40 #1 (25 Red + 175 White) #2 (50 Red + 150 White) #3 (75 Red + 125 White) #4 (100 Red + 100 White) #5 (125 Blue + 75 White) #6 (150 Blue + 50 White) #7 (175 Blue + 25 White) #8 200 MAX 1 x 400 (50 Free/50 Non-Free) 8 x 50 KICK D1-4, 5-8 to MAX @ 1:00

WEEK 26	Fri Feb 23 2024
WARMUP	4 x 200 IM-NonFree-Free-Kick 6 x 25 Build @ :30
SPRINT	3 x 200 Free @ 2:30 D1-3 4 x (100 red + 50 white) 4 x (50 MAX + 50 white)

DISTANCE	4 x {
	  1 x 75 MAX
	  (:30)
	  50 MAX from push
	}
	
	1 x 300 Easy
	2 x 200 @ 2:30
	White-Pink
	8 x 25 w/fins Underwater @ :40

MID-DISTANCE	4 x 200 #1-2 IM Descend, #2-4 Ascend Free 6 x 200 @ 2:30/2:50 #1-2 200 Pink – 25 Blue #3-4 200 Red – 25 MAX #5-6 200 Red – 25 Red max of 2 breaths 10 x (100 + 50 easy) Goal 1000 Pace 10 x (50 + 50 easy) Goal 500 Pace

WEEK 26	Sat Feb 24 2024

WARMUP	1 x 600 (300 Free-300 NonFree) 4 x 100 IMO (drill fly) @ :10 rest 8 x 50 (Fly/Free, Back/Free, Breast/Free, Free/Free) @ 6 x 75 (Kick/drill/swim) @ 1:10 8 x 25 @ :30 odds: drill/ evens: stroke 3 x 400 IM w/fins Fly & Free - BP: 3,5 by 50 @ 6:30 3 x 100 Fly/Back/BR @ 1:20

MAIN SET	2 x {
	   3 x 200 Paddle w/Pull Buoy
	   6 x 100 @ 1:05/1:10/1:15
	}

FEBRUARY · ELITE SWIM WORKOUT '24 · WEEK 27

Monday	Tuesday	Wednesday	Thursday	Friday	Saturday

1 x 200 Kick Breast
1 x 200 Kick Fly
1 x 200 Back
1 x 200 Kick Free
 	
3 x (w/fins
25 underwater kick @ :30
50 Fly descend @ :40
75 Fast Kick - Flutter @ 1:00/1:10
100 FAST @ 2:00
)
 	
SPRINT
1 x 300 Work each breakout
 	
3 x {
1 x 100 MAX @ 7:00
2 x 50 MAX @ 4:00
}
1 x 500 Free @ :20
5 x 50 Non-Free @ :50
1 x 400 Build each 100 to MAX finish @ :20
4 x 50 Non-Free @ :50
 	
DISTANCE
3 x {
1 x 300 Red (1:00)
1 x 200 Red (:30)
1 x 50 Red (2:00)
}
1 x 200 cool down
 	
MID-DISTANCE
5 x (400 @ 4:30/4:45/4:50 + 4 x 100 Goal 500 Pace @ 1:10/1:15/1:20 + 1:00 rest)
		200 SKIMPS
		1 x 500 Kick
		
		8 x 50 @ 1:00
		Each one work one flip turns pushing off on back
		4 x 100 JMI @ 1:10/1:15
		#1-2 Neg Split (White/Red)
		#2-4 DPS
		
		SPRINT
		3 x 200 w/fins DPS @ 2:30
		
		8 x 200 @ 2:40
		#1 (25 Red + 175 White)
		#2 (50 Red + 150 White)
		#3 (75 Red + 125 White)
		#4 (100 Red + 100 White)
		#5 (125 Blue + 75 White)
		#6 (150 Blue + 50 White)
		#7 (175 Blue + 25 White)
		#8 200 MAX
		
		1 x 400 (50 Free/50 Non-Free)
		8 x 50 KICK D1-4, 5-8 to MAX @ 1:00
		DISTANCE
		
		8 x 50 (25 Drill/ 25 build to max finish) @ :50
		
		1 x 400 BP- 3,5 by 100's @ 4:10
		4 x 50 Non-Free @ :50
		1 x 300 BP- 3,5,7 @ 3:50
		4 x 50 kick no board @ 1:00
		1 x 200 Kick Pink @ 4:00
		4 x 50 D 1-4 to Pink @ 1:00
		
		8 x 25 Breakout
		
		MID-DISTANCE
		4 x 500 @ 6:00/6:10
		1 white, 1 pink, 2 red
		5 x 300 RED @ 3:50
		12 x 50 D 1-6, 7-12 to MAX @ :50
			500 Choice
			200 Kick
			200 IM
			
			1 x 400 (100 Free/100 Non-Free/100 Kick no board/100 Free/100 Non Free)
			8 x 75 (Free/Non-Free/Drill) @ 1:10
			
			1 x 400 Kick
			
			4 x 200
			odds: Free @ 2:20/2:30
			evens: Stroke 2:30/2:40/2:50
			8 x 50
			odds: Free RB-2 @ :45
			evens: non-free @ 1:00
			
			300 (100 back/100 Choice/100 breast)
				3 x 200
				#1 Free
				#2 (50 BK/50 Breast)
				#3 DPS Choice
				
				5 x 100 (Kick/Drill/Swim/Drill) @ 2:00
				1 x 400 IMO w/Fins
				4 x 25 underwater kick @ :30
				
				SPRINT
				
				2 x (
				2 x 200 @ 3:00
				)
				6 x 100 Descend , Hold time on 5-6 @ 1:20/1:30
				6 x 50 Kick @ :50/:55
				4 x 50 @ 3:30 MAX
				2 x 400 @ 5:00/5:10
				
				DISTANCE
				3 x (300 + 100 easy)
				#1 Paddle/Pull White
				#2 Paddle Pink
				#3 Swim Red
				
				4 x (200 + 100 easy)
				White-Pink-Red-Blue
				5 x (100 + 50 easy)
				#1 Stroke D1-5 to MAX
				
				3 x 200 Paddle DPS @ 2:20/2:25
				
				MID-DISTANCE
				
				8 x 50 build to great finish @ 1:00
				
				10 x 100 @ 1:30 Best Average
				2 x Broken 500
				1 x 100 Red @ 1:40
				1 x 200 Pink @ 2:40
				1 x 100 Blue @ 1:40
				1 x 100 MAX @ 1:40	

WEEK 27	Mon Feb 26 2024

WARMUP	1 x 200 Kick Breast
	1 x 200 Kick Fly
	1 x 200 Back
	1 x 200 Kick Free
	3 x { w/fins
	   25 underwater kick @ :30
	   50 Fly descend @ :40
	   75 Fast Kick - Flutter @ 1:00/1:10
	   100 FAST @ 2:00
	   }

SPRINT	1 x 300 Work each breakout
	3 x {
	1 x 100 MAX @ 7:00
	2 x 50 MAX @ 4:00
	}
	1 x 500 Free @ :20
	5 x 50 Non-Free @ :50
	1 x 400 Build each 100 to MAX finish @ :20
	4 x 50 Non-Free @ :50

DISTANCE	3 x {
	   1 x 300 Red
	   (1:00)
	   1 x 200 Red
	   (:30)
	   1 x 50 Red
	   (2:00)
	    }
	
	1 x 200 cool down

MID-DISTANCE	5 x (400 @ 4:30/4:45/4:50 4 x 100 Goal 500 Pace @ 1:10/1:15/1:20 1:00 rest)

WEEK 27	Tue Feb 27 2024
WARMUP	4 x 200 IM 3 x 100 Freestyle 1 x 200 Kick 8 x 50 @ 1:00 Each one work one flip turns pushing off on back 4 x 100 JMI @ 1:10/1:15 #1-2 Neg Split (White/Red) #2-4 DPS
MAIN SET	Fly 5 x 100 Neg Split @ 1:30 5 x (200 @ 2:40/2:50 + 3 x 100 @ 1:30) 4 x 50 MAX kick dolphin on back @ 1:00

WEEK 27	Wed Feb 28 2024
WARMUP	200 SKIMPS 1 x 500 Kick 8 x 50 @ 1:00 Each one work one flip turns pushing off on back 4 x 100 JMI @ 1:10/1:15 #1-2 Neg Split (White/Red) #2-4 DPS
SPRINT	3 x 200 w/fins DPS @ 2:30 8 x 200 @ 2:40 #1 (25 Red + 175 White) #2 (50 Red + 150 White) #3 (75 Red + 125 White) #4 (100 Red + 100 White) #5 (125 Blue + 75 White) #6 (150 Blue + 50 White) #7 (175 Blue + 25 White) #8 200 MAX 1 x 400 (50 Free/50 Non-Free) 8 x 50 KICK D1-4, 5-8 to MAX @ 1:00
DISTANCE	8 x 50 (25 Drill/ 25 build to max finish) @ :50 1 x 400 BP: 3,5 by 100's @ 4:10 4 x 50 Non-Free @ :50 1 x 300 BP: 3,5,7 @ 3:50 4 x 50 kick no board @ 1:00 1 x 200 Kick Pink @ 4:00 4 x 50 D 1-4 to Pink @ 1:00 8 x 25 Breakout
MID-DISTANCE	4 x 500 @ 6:00/6:10 1 white, 1 pink, 2 red 5 x 300 RED @ 3:50 12 x 50 D 1-6 , 7-12 to MAX @ :50

WEEK 27	Thu Feb 29 2024
WARMUP	500 Choice 200 Kick 200 IM 1 x 400 (100 Free / 100 Non-Free / 100 Kick no board / 100 Free / 100 Non Free) 8 x 75 (Free / Non-Free / Drill) @ 1:10 1 x 400 Kick
MAIN SET	4 x 200 odds: Free @ 2:20 / 2:30 evens: Stroke 2:30 / 2:40 / 2:50 8 x 50 odds: Free RB:2 @ :45 evens: non-free @ 1:00 300 (100 back / 100 Choice / 100 breast)

WEEK 27	Fri Mar 01 2024
WARMUP	3 x 200 #1 Free #2 (50 BK/50 Breast) #3 DPS Choice 5 x 100 (Kick/Drill/Swim/Drill) @ 2:00 1 x 400 IMO w/Fins 4 x 25 underwater kick @ :30

SPRINT	2 x {
	   2 x 200 @ 3:00
	}
	6 x 100 Descend , Hold time on 5-6 @ 1:20/1:30
	6 x 50 Kick @ :50/:55
	
	4 x 50 @ 3:30 MAX
	2 x 400 @ 5:00/5:10

DISTANCE	3 x (300 + 100 easy) #1 Paddle/Pull White #2 Paddle Pink #3 Swim Red 4 x (200 + 100 easy) White-Pink-Red-Blue 5 x (100 + 50 easy) #1 Stroke D1-5 to MAX 3 x 200 Paddle DPS @ 2:20/2:25
MID-DISTANCE	8 x 50 build to great finish @ 1:00 10 x 100 @ 1:30 Best Average 2 x Broken 500 1 x 100 Red @ 1:40 1 x 200 Pink @ 2:40 1 x 100 Blue @ 1:40 1 x 100 MAX @ 1:40

GOALS AND NOTES

GOALS AND NOTES

GOALS AND NOTES

GOALS AND NOTES

GOALS AND NOTES

GOALS AND NOTES

GOALS AND NOTES

GOALS AND NOTES

GOALS AND NOTES

GOALS AND NOTES

Check out these other exciting titles!

A Novel **WOLVES OF WAR**

Nicaragua, 1975.

An elite squad of special forces soldiers secretly undertake covert operations on behalf of the United States. Times are changing, however, and the political climate of Nicaragua begins to take a step away from dictatorship and towards revolution, with the team caught in the center of it all.

With the sudden explosive arrival of a mysterious female doctor and a deadly assassin, the team realize a grave threat is lurking on the horizon, an enemy who will send everything they know and love into chaos.

As the stakes continue to rise, they realize they are fighting for more than just their lives - they are fighting to preserve their own humanity.

WHEN THE LINES OF RIGHT AND WRONG ARE BLURRED, HOW FAR WOULD YOU GO TO FIGHT FOR WHAT YOU BELIEVE IN?

Printed in Great Britain
by Amazon

37151885R00117